THE CAHUILLA INDIANS

BOOKS BY HARRY C. JAMES

The Treasure of the Hopitu

Haliksai! A Book of Legends of the Grand Canyon Country

The Hopi Indians

Red Man—White Man

The Cahuilla Indians

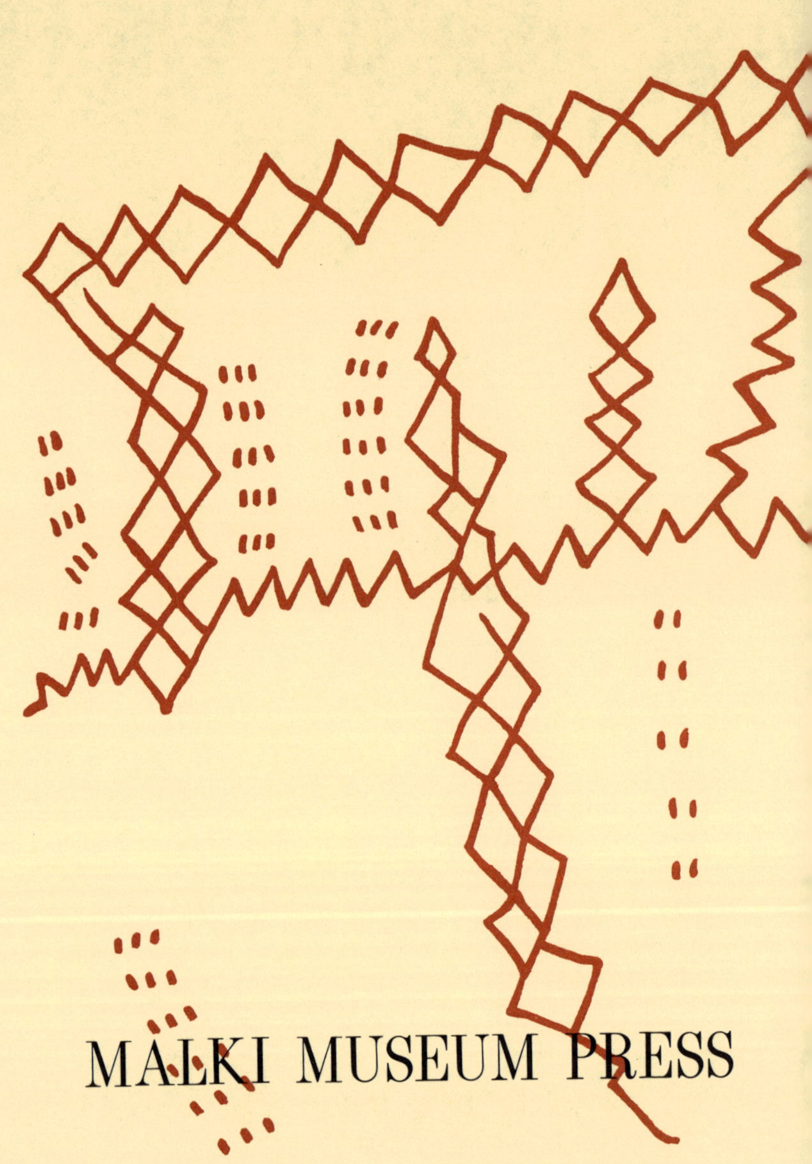

MALKI MUSEUM PRESS

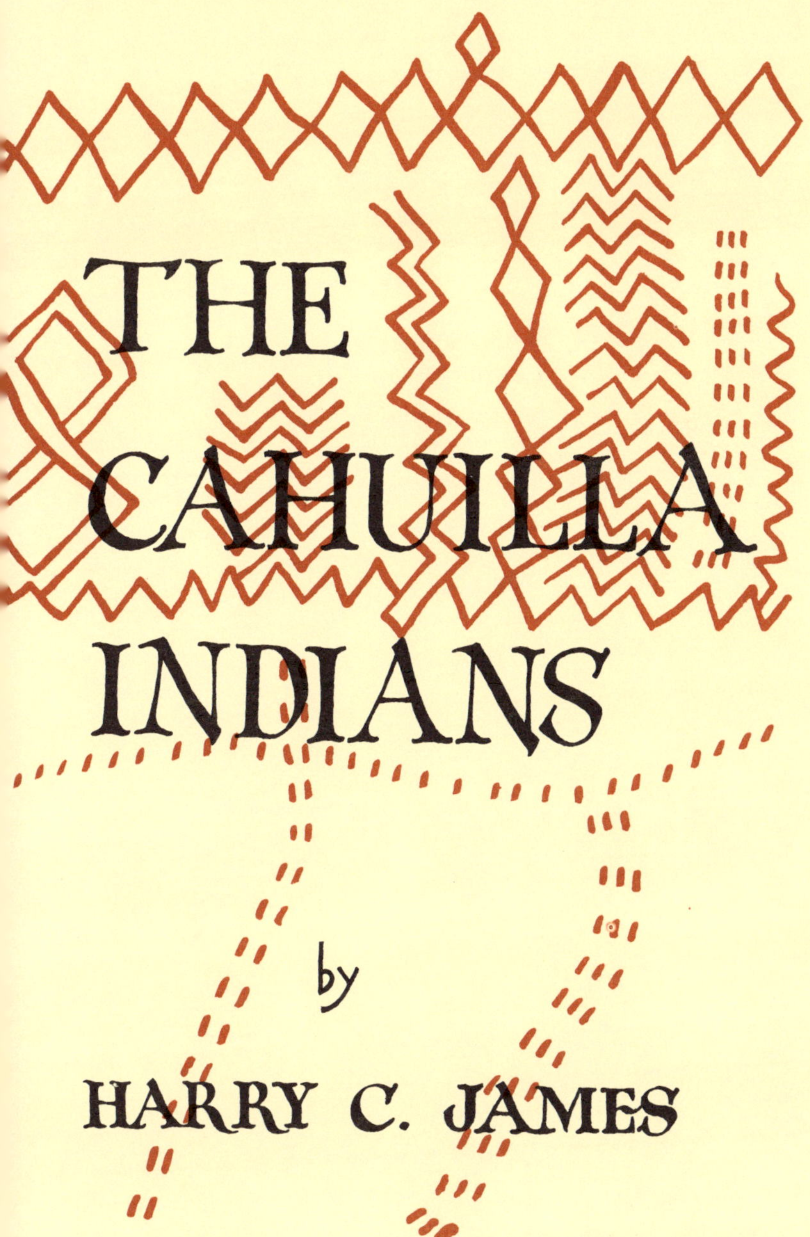

THE CAHUILLA INDIANS

by

HARRY C. JAMES

Library of Congress Catalog No. 60-10491

Photo-offset Lithography by
Rubidoux Printing Company, Riverside, California
PRINTED IN THE UNITED STATES OF AMERICA

Again for Grace

ACKNOWLEDGMENTS

THE AUTHOR WISHES TO ACknowledge his indebtedness to the authorities whose books are listed in the bibliography and to the many Cahuilla Indians who patiently answered all his questions and permitted him to make photographs whenever and wherever he pleased.

Many other persons have been unfailingly cooperative, particularly Dr. Clarence E. Smith, Director of the Palm Springs Desert Museum, who carefully read many sections of the manuscript and offered helpful suggestions for its improvement, and Dr. Charles E. Rozaire of the Southwest Museum, who took considerable time to locate and copy many invaluable old photographs from the Museum's extensive collection.

The staff of the Banning Library gave very material assistance by getting essential books from a variety of cooperating libraries.

Suggestions and help of one kind or another were graciously given by Mr. George R. Barker, Mr. Chester K. Hendricks, Mrs. Harry F. Hunt, and Mr. and Mrs. Francis J. Johnston of Banning, Mr. L. Burr Belden of San Bernardino and Mr. Gerald A. Smith of the San Bernardino County Museum, Mr. Frank M. Bogert, Mrs. J. Smeaton Chase, and Miss Cornelia B. White of Palm Springs, Dr. John P. Harrington of the Bureau of American Ethnology, Mr. Harry Hofmann, the late Mr. Arthur Tripp, and Mr. Charles Van Fleet of San Jacinto, Mr. Arthur Grant Evans of Pasadena, Dr. Mark R. Harrington of the Southwest Museum, Mr. Harry Lawton of Riverside, Dr. Horace Parker of Balboa Island, and Mrs. Nina Paul Shumway of Palm Desert.

CONTENTS

ILLUSTRATIONS

FOREWORD

Only occasionally does a book join the literature of the American Indian which combines the scholarly concern and the personal affection and warmth towards a people that permeate Harry C. James' *The Cahuilla Indian*. Utilizing published anthropological and historical studies and accounts related to him by individual Cahuilla, Mr. James has reconstructed the circumstances of life among this Southern California group prior to their contact with alien cultures.

Initially, Mr. James surveyed the literature thoroughly to provide an ethnographic framework for his book based on the works of anthropologists who studied the Cahuilla from the 1890's through the 1920's. The ethnographic data, however, did not provide him with as detailed or as human a picture of the culture as he desired. He therefore talked at length with many Cahuilla of different generations to learn more about their culture and history. As a consequence, his book makes its own significant contribution with some new ethnographical and historical material.

Not only does James present Cahuilla culture in clearer focus than many earlier works, writing in a style intelligible to the layman, but he also destroys many of the myths that have accumulated around such prominent Cahuilla leaders in California history as Juan Antonio, Antonio Garra, Ramona, and Fig Tree John.

His most impressive contribution, however, lies in the last chapter of the book. Nowhere else in the extensive literature of recent years on the Cahuilla are the conditions of modern-day life so well presented. The relation of the non-Cahuilla society with which they interact and the role of the Bureau of Indian Affairs in today's activities are fairly evaluated.

Since this book was completed in 1959, scholars have arrived at new interpretations of various aspects of Cahuilla culture and there have been many changes in the present-day life of this people. Articles have appeared with somewhat different analyses of the nature of Cahuilla social structure, and there have been more intensive evaluations of aboriginal institutions. These new studies can be found by consulting the Cahuilla bibliography cited in the slightly revised bibliography on page 184 of this new edition.

The circumstances of modern Cahuilla life have altered significantly since the appearance of this book. Educational opportunities and goals of the young Cahuilla people have expanded. A college education is now a reality for some Cahuilla and scholarship programs emanating from the Cahuilla themselves are aiding young people in enlarging their horizons. Malki Museum and the American Indian Historical Society have both been active in the educational area. More and more Cahuilla are becoming involved in scholarly and educational pursuits. Mrs. Jane Penn, a director of Malki Museum, has worked not only to preserve the heritage of her people but to interest non-Indians in native culture. Mrs. Katherine Saubel has co-authored several scholarly works. Mr. Rupert Costo, a Cahuilla and descendant of Juan Antonio, is editor-in-chief of the *Indian Historian* and president of the American Indian Historical Society.

The relations between the Cahuilla people and non-Indians are also changing rapidly. The scandalous legal exploitation of the Cahuillas of Palm Springs has recently been exposed through the efforts of the Cahuilla and a Pulitzer Prize-winning series in the Riverside Press-Enterprise. The Cahuillas are demanding and securing the right to make their own decisions about their present and future. Today, they are becoming more and more active at every level of Indian affairs from the local to national scene. Cahuillas are also working with non-Indians to a greater extent than ever before in the past, participating in local community matters, statewide political organizations, and in social and scholarly activities. Their spirit today is characterized by a deep and abiding interest in their past and an aggressive grasp for the future.

In reprinting this new edition of *The Cahuilla Indians* in both hardcover and paperback, Malki Museum Press wishes to express its extreme gratitude to Paul Bailey, publisher of Westernlore Press, who kindly consented to the reprint of a book which appeared originally as Volume XVIIIof the Great West and Indian Series of Westernlore publications. The new edition has been printed by photo-offset lithography from the original press sheets. A number of minor changes have been made, including the substitution of several photographs as requested by the author and the addition of a number of items to the bibliography. The cover or dustjacket illustration of Chief Cabezon, the noted Cahuilla leader, is from a photograph taken in the late nineteenth century by C. C. Pierce. We are grateful to the Henry E. Huntington Library of San Marino for permission to use the photograph and to Edwin H. Carpenter of that library's staff who helped in the search for photographic materials.

Personally, I should like to recognize the efforts of other members of the Malki Museum Publications Committee besides myself in making this reprint possible, including Harry W. Lawton, chairman, and Mrs. Katherine Saubel. In addition, Mrs. Wistaria Linton provided

photographic advice, the original illustrator Don Perceval contributed
design ideas, and Vernon Tegland of Rubidoux Printers spearheaded
the printing.

Finally, I wish to pay tribute to those Cahuilla people who
originally contributed to this book in many ways and who since its
first publication in 1960 have passed on: Victoria Wierick, Salvador
Lopez, Calistro Tortes, Harry Hopkins, Louis Levi, and Calistro Lugo.

Lowell John Bean
California State College, Hayward

I

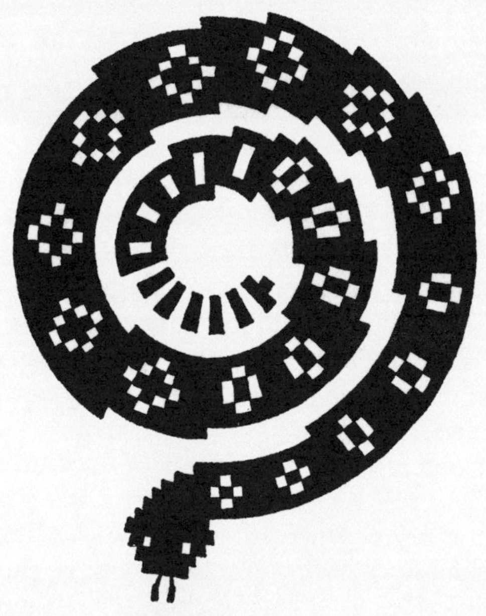

THE INFLUENCE OF THE NATIVE Indian upon the state of California is obvious at once to even the most casual visitor. Thirteen California counties bear Indian names—Colusa, Inyo, Marin, Modoc, Mono, Napa, Shasta, Siskiyou, Sonoma, Tehama, Tuolumne, Yolo, Yuba. From the Oregon to the Mexican border, from the Arizona and Nevada boundaries to the Pacific Ocean, the map of the Golden State is dotted with names of Spanish-Indian origin.

Of the multitude of Indian groups indigenous to southern California the Cahuilla Indians are responsible for more place names than any other group. Even well beyond the limits of Cahuilla territory there are towns, schools, and streets with names of Cahuilla or Spanish-Cahuilla origin or association. Tahquitz, Ramona, Alessandro, Patencio, Arenas, and Juan Diego are typical.

The meaning of the word Cahuilla is obscure. The "Scotch Paisano," Hugo Reid, claimed that it means "master." Dr. David Prescott Barrows also gave to the word the meaning of "master," or "ruling one," or "powerful man." To this day the Cahuilla often speak of one of their leaders as having *power*. By this they do not mean physical strength, but mental and spiritual strength—strength of character.

The word is sometimes spelled "Coahuila," and this spelling was ruled as official in 1933 in the Sixth Report of the United States Bureau of Geographic Names. No one seems to know how or why this spelling came about, as early maps all carried it as "Cahuilla." The name has been variously applied to two mountains, Mount Cahuilla and Little Cahuilla, Cahuilla Valley, Cahuilla Indian Reservation, the village of Cahuilla which once existed near present-day Anza, and Lake Cahuilla, the large freshwater or brackish lake which in the past covered much of Coachella and Imperial Valleys and was the ancestor of the Salton Sea.

The Cahuilla can even claim the distinction of having "written" an American college song! It seems that Dr. David Prescott Barrows and a Professor Brackett were greatly intrigued by the melody and rhythm of a song which they had heard at a Cahuilla ceremonial. They wrote some humorous words for the "tune" and the song became popular among their friends. Later other words were written and the result, entitled "The Torch Bearers," became the traditional song of Pomona College. It is used at Commencement and on other special occasions there. Published by H. W. Gray of New York, it has become widely known as one of the most interesting of American college songs.

The Cahuilla names on the land of southern California are significant of the part these Indians played here in the past, and are continuing to play. Museums are rich with their artifacts. The names of many of their chiefs are prominent in history. Cahuilla adults live and work among us. Cahuilla children attend our public schools. Cahuilla problems concerning land and water give rise to frequent newspaper headlines. Their highly photogenic palm oases in the desert canyons of the Mecca-Indio Hills and the Santa Rosa and San Jacinto Mountains are often seen in current motion pictures, to say nothing of their value as tourist attractions and as retreats for those who find true recreation in places of rare natural beauty.

Who are these so-called Cahuilla Indians? What is their history? What of their culture?—their religion? What was and is their way of life? What does the future hold for them?

CONSIDERABLE CONTACT
with the Cahuilla Indians and a careful reading of the published record regarding them—a very scanty record it is, unfortunately—compels us to conclude that these natives of the deserts and mountains of southern California are a much maligned people. Even the most casual reading of what accounts we can consider accurate is bound to convince us that they are far from the docile,

degraded "diggers" which only too frequently they have been represented to be.

Possibly the best index to Cahuilla intelligence and imagination is their folk-lore, highly poetic and broadly cosmic in concept. Any thoughtful examination of their artifacts also proves that intelligent and imaginative minds guided their hands, and, further, that they were by no means afraid of work. To shape from solid granite manos and pestles and metates and mortars with the symmetry and finish which many of their specimens show requires craftsmanship of a high order and unstinting labor. To make pottery as graceful as are many of their ollas, and baskets as beautiful in design as theirs are, demonstrates intelligence, artistry, and industry.

Still further evidence of Cahuilla intelligence is to be found in their exceptionally apt adaptation to living in the environmental extremes of their habitat. High in the valleys of the San Jacinto-Santa Rosa Mountains, 4000 to 5000 feet and more *above* sea level, the Mountain Cahuilla had to contend with winter cold and snow. At the other climatic extreme, in the desert reaches of the Salton Sea area, in some places 200 feet *below* the level of the sea, the Desert Cahuilla had to battle drought and sand and heat. In the open canyons and valleys of San Gorgonio Pass the Western Cahuilla had to adjust their living to the fierce winds and the inordinate fluctuations in temperature which are marked features of the Pass.

Very early the Cahuilla were enriched by the blood and culture of other southern California Indians. Cupeño from the Warner's Ranch area and Serrano from the nearby San Bernardinos for one reason or another came to live among the Cahuilla at various times. They brought with them cultural influences which gradually merged into the fabric of the folklore and ceremonial life of the Cahuilla.

"Mission Indians," the Gabrieleño and the Luiseño and the Diegueño—named for the Spanish missions to which they were subject—on many occasions sought refuge among the isolated Cahuilla from the cruelties and indignities inflicted upon them by the Spaniards, by the Mexicans, and by the early American pioneers.

The Hugo Reid, referred to in Chapter I, was a well-educated Scot who married the daughter of a one-time chief of the Gabrieleño Indians. In 1852 he wrote a series of letters to the *Los Angeles Star* in which he commented very frankly upon the treatment meted out to Indian neophytes under San Gabriel Mission control. He described how Indians who attempted to desert and were caught were subjected to whipping with "immense scourges of rawhide ten feet long," and how, if they persisted in their attempts to escape, they were branded on the lip or had an ear chopped off to make identification easier. He spoke highly of the gentleness, the intelligence, and the law-abiding character of these Indians before they were destroyed by this process of character assassination—under the guise of conversion to the gentle precepts of Christ.

To such unhappy victims, the mountain valleys and the far desert lands of the Cahuilla must have seemed a haven indeed.

Hard as was the lot of Mission Indians under the Spaniards it became even more desperate under Mexican and, later, under frontier American jurisdiction. Major Horace Bell in his colorful *Reminiscences of a Ranger*, published in 1881, writes in great detail of the near slavery into which the last remnants of the Los Angeles Mission Indians had been forced when he arrived in that then tiny city in the 1850's. Let one of his graphic accounts speak for itself.

"About sundown the pompous marshal, with his special Indian deputies, who had been kept in jail all day to keep them sober, would drive and drag the herd [of Indians] to a big corral in the rear of Downey Block, where they would sleep away their intoxication, and in the morning they would be exposed for sale, as slaves for the week. Los Angeles had its slave mart, as well as New Orleans and Constantinople—only the slave at Los Angeles was sold fifty-two times a year as long as he lived, which did not generally exceed one, two, or three years, under the new dispensation. They would be sold for a week, and bought up by the vineyard men and others at prices ranging from one to three dollars, one-third of which was to be paid to the peon at the end of the week, which debt, due for well performed labor, would invariably be paid in *aguardiente*, and the Indian would be made happy until the following Monday morning, having passed through another Saturday night and Sunday's saturnalia of debauchery and bestiality. Those thousands of honest, useful people were absolutely destroyed in this way. . . .

"Surely, we civilized the race of Mission Indians with a refinement known to no other people under the sun."

Dr. S. F. Cook comments at length on the sad plight of the Indian in the Anglo-American system in his carefully documented *The Conflict Between the California Indian and White Civilization* (Ibero-Americana No. 23, University of California Press, 1943). This system, he says, "had in it no place for the Indian. If the latter could by his own initiative find subsistence within its framework, there was a priori nothing to prevent such an adjustment. But if there was any conflict whatsoever with the system, the native was to be eliminated ruthlessly, either by outright extermination or by the slower method of segregation in ghetto-like reservations."

Earlier (Ibero-Americana No. 21) he pointed out that "the type of disciplinary measures was frequently degrading and offensive to the Indian. Corporeal punishment, or flogging, was of course standard practice in the eighteenth century among all white civilizations, particularly when used upon so-called inferior races. Nevertheless it was singularly ineffective, for unless the physical effects are so terrific as to break down utterly the spirit of a man, the result is usually to inspire him with an undying, implacable hatred, which in turn communicates itself to all his friends. Imprisonment, or other curtailment of liberty, if properly carried out, does not result in bodily harm, and is much more dreaded by a race to whom freedom means the breath of life. It was therefore unfortunate that the lash was so quickly resorted to by the Spanish administration and applied with such severity."

From 1850 to 1855 the California legislature passed three laws which legalized what was virtually an American version of the Spanish-Mexican peon system. One of these laws denied to the Indians the right to testify in court. Another decreed that any Indian, upon the word of a white citizen, could be brought into court and declared a vagrant. Then he could be put up at auction and sold as a laborer to the highest bidder for a period of four months without compensation other than his keep. As any unemployed Indian could easily be proved a vagrant he really, in many instances, became not a peon but a slave. The third law decreed that any Indian adult or child (without consent of his parents) could be bound over to a white citizen for a term of years, being paid for his labor only in subsistence. Laws such as these were used to every advantage by unscrupulous whites and incredible hardship was wrought upon the Indian victims.

In making a comparison of the California Indian population under the three different regimes Dr. Cook concluded that it had been reduced seventy-two percent under Spain, thirty-one percent during the Mexican period after the secularization of the missions, and eighty-two percent under the American rule from 1848 to 1880.

The plight of California Indians in general eventually became something of a national scandal. Helen Hunt Jackson published in 1881 *A Century of Dishonor* and followed it in 1884 with her novel, *Ramona*. *Ramona* became a red man's *Uncle Tom's Cabin* and aroused a wave of indignation throughout the country which further spurred Mrs. Jackson's crusade to secure justice for the Indian. Incidentally, it is likely that *Ramona's* glowing picture of life in California during the Mission period did more than the Gold Rush to step up migration to the Golden State.

In 1882 Mrs. Jackson and Mr. Abbott Kinney, a highly intelligent, public-spirited pioneer promoter of California, had been appointed to make a report to the then Commissioner of Indian Affairs on the condition of the Indians of southern California. This report, made in 1883, makes several references to the Cahuilla and gives us our most authentic picture of the tribe as of that date.

By that time there were few Mission Indians left and those few were living in shacks in wasteland slums near the major white settlements. Mrs. Jackson writes of the contrast between these poor sodden wretches and the mountain Cahuilla who were living in industrious, peaceful communities happily "cultivating ground, keeping stock, carrying on their own simple manufactures of pottery, mats, baskets, etc., and making their living—a very poor living, it is true; but they are independent and self-respecting in it and ask nothing of the United States Government now, except that it will protect them in the ownership of their lands."

Mrs. Jackson goes on to write of their pride, of their refusal to beg even when they had been brought close to starvation by crop failure. She found them neatly dressed, their faces animated with intelligence, the children good students in the small schools which had been established for them.

Mrs. Jackson and Mr. Kinney did not themselves visit the Western and the Desert Cahuilla, but they sent a Captain J. G. Stanley, a former Indian agent, in whom they had trust, to represent them. Captain Stanley held a meeting with about one hundred Cahuilla Indians from eight different village groups which seemed to be more or less dominated by old Chief Cabazon. (Captain Stanley estimated that Cabazon was then at least one hundred years old—but are not all old Indian chiefs automatically one hundred years old?) Stanley reports that these Cahuilla were not considered Christians and that they still were following their ancient customs and religions.

It is interesting to find in this report a statement from a committee from "the small white settlement called Banning" with regard to either the Western Cahuilla or the Serrano—the statement is not clear on this point. The statement speaks of an Indian community in the region called *The Potrero* and of what a fine example it is of an industrious little settlement with good land, well-fenced and under cultivation. In passing, it is interesting to note that Dr. Welwood Murray, well-known Palm Springs pioneer, was a member of the Banning committee referred to.

Certainly the Cahuilla were fortunate in being isolated from the sadistic barbarities of the early Spanish, Mexican, and American periods. It is true that as American pioneers pushed farther and farther inland and higher and higher into the mountain valleys of Cahuilla territory many tragic and unfortunate incidents occurred. The killing in cold blood of the Cahuilla Juan Diego by Sam Temple, who thought that possibly the Indian had stolen his horse—the incident that Helen Hunt Jackson used in the tragic climax of *Ramona*—shows that even in the 1880's the frontier concept that the only good Indian is a dead Indian had not yet been obliterated.

However, with the coming of more and more Americans into the West, the crude brutalities of earlier days gradually vanished. Many of the whites who came into contact with the Cahuilla in constantly greater numbers were either friendly and interested in the Indians or at least willing to treat them with some degree of consideration.

Eventually, lands were set aside as reservations for the Cahuilla. Reservation boundaries were finally definitely established and no longer were "floated" hither and yon to the satisfaction of some settler desirous of securing a valuable water right or a particularly fertile piece of land.

The intelligence, the honesty, and the upright individuality of the Cahuilla won them many friends and stalwart supporters. Writers J. Smeaton Chase, George Wharton James, Charles Fletcher Lummis, Charles Francis Saunders and artist Karl Eytel all knew the Cahuilla well and always spoke of them most highly. During the years of her retirement in New Mexico, Miss Clara True, one-time Indian agent at Banning, often spoke with affection and admiration of the Cahuilla who had been in her charge. She found them quite a handful to manage, but she certainly liked them!

In 1897 a young anthropologist at the University of Chicago offered as a thesis for his Ph.D. a monograph entitled "The Ethno-Botany of the Coahuilla *(sic!)* Indians of Southern California." This budding scientist was David Prescott Barrows, later for many years president of the University of California. His studies awoke in him a lifelong interest in and admiration for this people, and to this day he is vividly and affectionately remembered by many aged Cahuilla, more than one of whom has said to us, "He lived with us as if he were one of us. His books can tell you all about us."

Except in one notable instance the Cahuilla generally seemed to have won the interest and respect of all the more intelligent persons who came in contact with them in the early days of California history. Only Father Pedro Font, diarist and chaplain of the de Anza expedition of 1775, wrote of the Cahuilla he saw in Coyote Canyon as being degraded savages, and California Indian music he described as "songs of hell." But then Father Font seems to have taken rather an unfortunate view of all Indians who had not been properly baptized into his own faith!

SCIENTISTS HAVE FOUND language roots to be the most effective basis for grouping the various aboriginal tribes of the Americas. According to this system of classification the Cahuilla Indians belong to the Shoshonean division of the Uto-Aztecan linguistic family. This group includes such diverse peoples as the Aztecs of Mexico, the Hopi and the Papago and the Pima of Arizona, the Ute of Colorado and Utah, as well as the neighboring tribes of the Cahuilla—the Gabriel-eño, the Luseño, the Cupeño, and the Serrano. However, it is wise to remember that a Ute or a Hopi would find the language of a Cahuilla entirely incomprehensible.

The languages of the Indians of California were, and still are, so diversified and so complex as to pose serious problems to all students of these languages. At least twenty-one linguistic groups are represented, giving force to Dr. Frederick Webb Hodge's statement that "California must probably be regarded as the region of the greatest aboriginal linguistic diversity in the world."

There were, to some extent, language differences not only among the three divisions of the Cahuilla tribe but also among the villages. This diversity in the native Cahuilla speech—plus the accretions added by refugees from other California tribes—has made the study of the language an interesting but rather frustrating experience for those who have attempted to puzzle out this Cahuilla babel. It is hoped that current studies of the language by Hansjacob Seiler and others may do much to clarify the present confusion.

Something of a mystery is the fact that, in spite of their relative isolation from the influence of the Franciscan missions, the Cahuilla adopted many Spanish personal names and many Spanish terms for articles in common use. Cahuilla names are indeed awkward for the English tongue and difficult for us to render phonetically. Perhaps the complexity of pattern in their language caused the Cahuilla to accept Spanish as a sort of convenient *lingua franca*. Dr. Clarence E. Smith, Director of the Palm Springs Desert Museum, suggests that the Cahuilla's acceptance and use of Spanish may have come because of its prestige value, just as "cultured" Americans like to throw into their casual conversation French words and phrases. We have come across Cahuilla toddlers who seemed to gain prestige satisfaction by speaking English in preference to their native tongue!

All three groups of Cahuilla Indians refer to their native language as *iviat* and to those who speak it as *iviatim*, and this seems to be one of the few basic linguistic points on which they all agree.

At this point it must be stressed that the Cahuilla were never really a "tribe" to the extent that that word is defined as meaning an independent political and linguistic group with definite territory of its own, comprising a number of smaller dependent groups all of which owe allegiance to one leader. Even the earliest records of the Cahuilla show them broken up into a multitude of small village groups, established wherever water and food were available.

Students of the Cahuilla generally consider them as made up of three divisions: Desert Cahuilla, Mountain Cahuilla, and Western (or Pass) Cahuilla. We prefer to use Western instead of Pass Cahuilla for we feel that the latter is a rather misleading term, since the Indians of this division were by no means limited to the area of San Gorgonio Pass. These three divisions are really rather loose geographic groupings of small independent villages or rancherias which differed from each other, to a degree, in speech and custom.

A reference to any of these three main groupings means little or nothing to a Cahuilla of today. If he is

CAHUILLA VILLAGE SITES

WESTERN CAHUILLA

1. Banning Water Canyon
2. Stubbe Canyon
3. Whitewater Canyon
4. Snow Creek
5. Blaisdell Canyon
6. Andreas Canyon
7. Chino Canyon
8. Tahquitz Canyon

WESTERN CAHUILLA
(Continued)

9. Deep Canyon
10. Palm Springs Station
11. Palm Springs
12. Indian Wells

CAHUILLA VILLAGE SITES

MOUNTAIN CAHUILLA

  I. San Ignacio
  II. San Ysidro
  III. Wiliya
  IV. Rockhouse Canyon
  V. Old Santa Rosa
  VI. Horse Canyon
  VII. Paui
  VIII. Cahuilla Mountain
  IX. Thomas Mountain
  X. Terwilliger Flats
  XI. Sahatapa

DESERT CAHUILLA

  A. Fish Springs
  B. Fig Tree John
  C. Agua Dulce
  D. Puichekiva
  E. La Mesa
  F. Torres Canyon
  G. Pushawalla Canyon
  H. Maswuut—Helaat
  I. Palaiyil

asked what "tribe" he belongs to he may reply with the name of the group with which his family has become affiliated, perhaps in fairly recent years. A Cahuilla living on the Morongo Reservation, for example, may give as an answer to the question the name of the ancient clan, say the *Wanikiktum,* to which his family belonged when it was located near where Whitewater is today. A Palm Springs Indian may speak of himself as belonging to the Agua Caliente "tribe." If pressed for details he may give you the name of one of the many Cahuilla clans, or, to make up for his lack of basic knowledge about his own people, he may accommodatingly tell his questioner whatever he presumes the questioner wants to know!

All this naturally has led to considerable confusion and disagreement among the whites interested in trying to understand the Cahuilla and among the Cahuilla themselves. The names of clan groups, these clan names in turn half-remembered, the names of certain clan sites—all tend to obscure rather than to clarify the Cahuilla picture. It is unfortunate that no real attempts to study these people were made until the various clans were disintegrating and much of the ceremonial lore and early history were forgotten.

We are indebted for what knowledge we have to such scientists as David Prescott Barrows, Lucile Hooper, A. L. Kroeber, and William Duncan Strong, who sifted painstakingly through the conflicting mass of fragmentary information about the Cahuilla and produced excellent foundation material on which to base later studies.

The Cahuilla developed their villages around springs, "Indian wells," or beside streams in the mountains and in desert canyons. They located them so as to take advantage of every local factor which could contribute to human comfort and convenience. The availability of water and of good food-gathering terrain were the essentials to be considered in the determining of a suitable village site. Protection from wind, warmth during the cold days of winter, shade during the hot days of summer, and even a fine regard for the natural beauty of the area were additional factors to which they gave thought.

Every Cahuilla village had very set boundaries. The territory in which its people lived, the area in which they could collect food, the range in which they could hunt were all very clearly defined. Because of the scarcity of food throughout the regions inhabited by the Cahuilla, disputes over these boundaries sometimes became very bitter. Indeed such disputes seem to have been the major if not the only cause of the few "wars" between the villages. Despite their reputation for independence and rugged integrity the Cahuilla seem to have been a peaceable people.

The inhabitants of each Cahuilla village belonged to one of two large societies: the Wild Cat and the Coyote —*Istam* and *Tuktum*. These two societies were subdivided into a multitude of clans, membership in the clan being through the father. Members of the Wild Cat Society were expected to marry into the Coyote Society, and vice versa.

Each clan usually had a ceremonial leader known as the *Net*. The Net was not only in charge of all the ceremonial procedures of his clan, but he also acted as judge and as executive officer in all matters pertaining to the general welfare of his clan. Matters of importance to the people of several clans were discussed in informal meetings of the clan Nets, or a sort of poll of the various Nets would be made by having a mesenger go to each Net and obtain his wishes as to the matter in controversy.

Each Net had a ceremonial house in which he lived and in which were centered the religious observances of the clan. This ceremonial building was known as *Kishumnawat*. In recent times it is more often spoken of as a "fiesta house," a "dance house," or simply "the big house."

The ceremonial house was usually circular, with the floor sunk a few inches below ground level. The roof was high-pitched and sloped steeply to the side walls, which were about four feet high. The roof beams were supported by upright forked posts well set in the earth. The whole structure was thatched with whatever material was available—palm fronds and arrow weed in the desert, wattled willow, tules, and other pliant shrubs in the mountains.

In more modern times the building is always rectangular, and wood, adobe, wattled palm fronds and corrugated iron may be used in its construction.

The houses in which the Cahuilla lived were called *Kish* and there was great variety in their construction. Many of them were simple circular brush shelters erected over scooped-out saucer-like depressions in the desert floor. An opening at the apex of the roof served as a smoke vent for the small fire that was used in the preparation of meals.

Some of their later houses were square or rectangular in shape, constructed on a pole frame-work. The walls were wattled and the roof thatched with tules or other suitable plants. In the desert regions where there was an abundance of native palms the leaves were used for both walls and roof. These houses were probably an architectural innovation stemming from Mexico where the modern *jacal* is almost identical to this later Cahuilla dwelling. As time went on Spanish-type adobe buildings replaced these more primitive structures, especially in areas where they proved more effective against inclement weather.

Where caves were available they too were used for dwellings. To make more commodious living quarters the Indians often built up a brush shelter in front of the cave. According to Calistro Tortes of Santa Rosa, the Cahuilla of the mountains also made shelters from slabs of incense cedar bark.

Besides the ceremonial house and the family dwelling each village might have one or more *hoyachat,* or sweat houses, where both men and women could take the sweat baths that so often were an important part of Indian life among the tribes of our western states. These sweat houses were brush structures from eight to twelve feet in diameter, well covered with earth.

Some Cahuilla villages had a structure called *tomekish,* similar to but larger than the sweat house. This seems to have been simply a general meeting place for the men of the village.

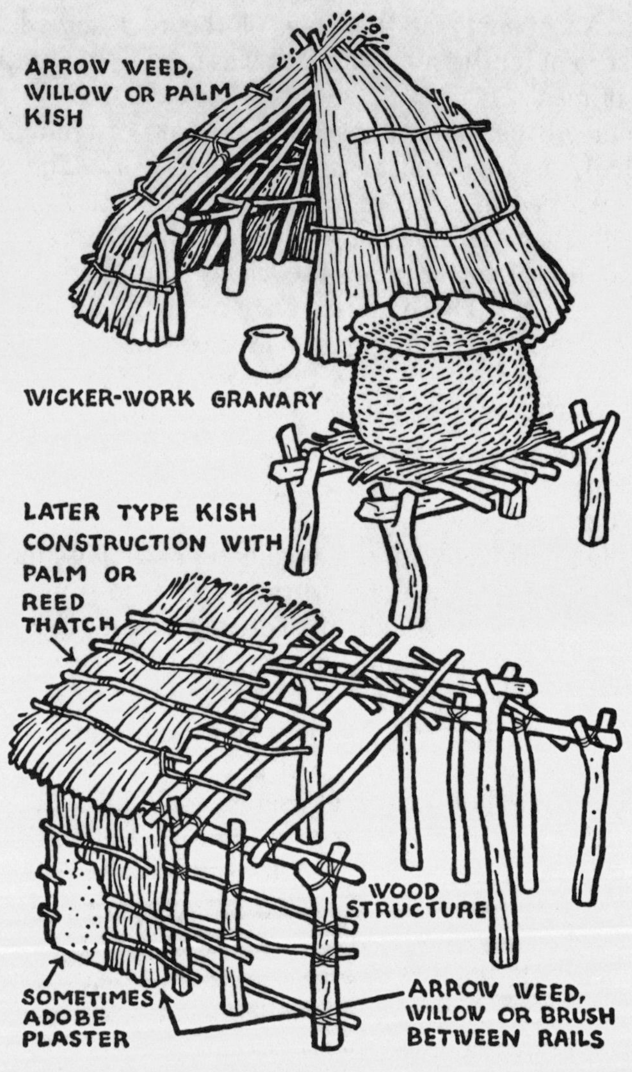

TYPES OF CAHUILLA DWELLINGS

On warm pleasant days the Cahuilla spent much time under the shade of *ramadas,* structures which also show Mexican influence. A ramada is an arbor made by setting in place four or more stout forked posts to carry a roof of poles and thatch.

A prominent feature of nearly every Cahuilla village were the well-constructed basket granaries. These were sometimes built on tops of square houses, sometimes on tops of special ramadas, and sometimes on a low platform of poles set on four, or six, or eight supporting posts. In these were stored acorns, mesquite beans, and a great variety of seeds, the gathering of which was a major activity of the Cahuilla—a subject that will be dealt with later.

Much confusion exists as to where the many Cahuilla villages were located. Much of this confusion is due to the fact that the Cahuilla had many temporary camping spots, places where they seasonally gathered seeds and plants, or hunted, or fished. And, of course, the invasion of the white man into Cahuilla territory made serious and permanent changes in many of the original Indian sites. The most complete account of the various Cahuilla village sites is to be found in William Duncan Strong's *Aboriginal Society in Southern California,* published in 1929 by the University of California. Many present-day Cahuilla, however, are not in complete agreement with Dr. Strong's paper.

Considerable delving into this controversial subject through much reading and many interviews leads us to feel that the paragraphs which follow locate, to the very best of our knowledge, the major original sites as they existed during the early days of the white man's occupancy of Cahuilla country.

The villages of the Western Cahuilla were in Banning Water Canyon; at the entrance to Stubbe,* Whitewater, Snow Creek, Blaisdell, Andreas, Chino, Tahquitz, and Deep Canyons; where the Palm Springs station is today; and around the hot springs in what is now Palm Springs. Anthropologists are rather generally agreed that the last-named village was the focal center of Western Cahuilla ceremonial life.

The village site at Indian Wells is considered by some authorities to have belonged to the Western Cahuilla. Others feel that it belonged to the Desert Cahuilla. The fact that the people there constructed the wells so typical of the Desert Cahuilla would seem to indicate that the people of Indian Wells were true Desert Cahuilla. On the other hand, certain clan and ceremonial relationships that existed there would lead one to believe that the village was part of the Western Cahuilla group.

The most southern village of the Mountain Cahuilla was at San Ignacio in San Diego County. The Mountain Cahuilla in this area had close contacts with the neighboring Cupeño and Diegueño tribes. At the village site at San Ysidro people of all three mingled to such an extent that we cannot consider San Ysidro a true Mountain Cahuilla village. In the Coyote Canyon area of the present Anza-Borrego State Park there was a Mountain Cahuilla village known as *Wiliya* around which were a number of widely scattered smaller villages.

*According to the desert old-timers Bill Keys and Johnny Lang, Stubbe Springs in Joshua Tree National Monument and Stubbe Canyon back of San Gorgonio Pass were both named after an old desert-rat who spelled his name that way. We understand that this is a rather common Scandinavian name meaning tree-stump.

46

In the high country of the Santa Rosa and San Jacinto Mountains occurred another grouping of Mountain Cahuilla sites. Three of them were on the shoulders of Toro and Santa Rosa Peak, two on a fork of Rock House Canyon at Old Santa Rosa and one at New Santa Rosa. About a half mile east of Horse Canyon there was still another village.

In the middle 1870's surviving Mountain Cahuilla from several broken clans gathered together around the warm springs about five miles west of Anza. There they established the village of *Paui* to which the whites in time gave the name of Cahuilla. This community became the center for all the older villages scattered throughout this extensive high mountain plateau, from the base of Mt. Cahuilla on the northwest and Thomas Mountain on the north to the large village at Terwilliger Flats on the southeast. Indeed, wherever there was a stream or a spring in these high mountain valleys and "flats" Mountain Cahuilla seem to have taken advantage of it, either to live there permanently or to camp there temporarily.

In the 1840's Juan Antonio, a leader of the Mountain Cahuilla, was persuaded to move several bands of his people into the vicinity of the present city of Riverside where they established a village. There they prepared to help the Mexican authorities to guard Cajon Pass against marauding Indians from the Colorado River region and from as far away as Utah.

Some time later they moved into San Timoteo Canyon and there, near the springs at present-day El Casco, they set up a village known as *Sahatapa*. A smallpox epidemic virtually wiped out this village and Juan Antonio himself fell victim to the disease. The remnants of this group eventually scattered out among the Western Cahuilla in the San Gorgonio Pass area, some even joining the bands at Palm Springs.

Juan Antonio was such an important character in California history that we shall devote full consideration to him later on.

The Desert Cahuilla lived on the floor of the Colorado Desert and near the beautiful palm oases along the base of the Indio and Mecca Hills. Villages were established wherever permanent water was available, either from natural water-holes or from the ingenious "Indian wells" that the Desert Cahuilla developed.

These wells were unique both in conception and in execution. So far as we know, no other tribe of North American Indians ever dug wells. Wherever there was a feeble spring or a seep the Desert Cahuilla, with great labor, would construct a long, narrow, open passageway to it, often with steps at the end down to the water.

J. Smeaton Chase, in his classic *California Desert Trails*, writes of these desert wells: "In the word or phrase applied to their ancient wells, now nonexistent, to which one descended by steps cut in the earth, we have an example of natural language-building. The Cahuilla word for a water-jar (Spanish, *olla*) is *ka-wo-mal*, and that for earth or ground, *te-mal*. Hence the well was *te-ma-ka-wo-mal* or earth-*olla*, neatly enough."

Recent aerial surveys by scientists have disclosed along the perimeter of the ancient lake called variously Blake's Sea, Lake Cahuilla, and Lake LeConte, a very large number of village sites. This once great lake evidently sup-

48

plied a very rich fish harvest to the Indians who lived there at that time. Scientists are now trying to determine whether those ancient Indians were ancestors of present-day Cahuilla or of some of the old populations of Baja California.

The most southerly of the Desert Cahuilla villages was located at Fish Springs near the northern end of Salton Sea. This village was called *Tuva* and it belonged to the clan of one of the best-known Cahuilla Indians, Fig Tree John.

We believe that Fig Tree John did not live at Tuva but near springs a few miles to the northwest. These springs later came to be known as Fig Tree John Springs and were so designated on the Geological Survey Map of the period. When this spot was flooded by the Salton Sea in the early 1900's Fig Tree John and his people moved to Agua Dulce Springs where they re-established their village. Unfortunately Agua Dulce Springs soon became known as Fig Tree John Springs, too, and this duplication of names has resulted in serious confusion in the identification of village sites in this particular area.

Probably the most important Desert Cahuilla village was the one called *Puichekiva*, Road Runner's House, located about seven miles south of Coachella. There a fine well furnished a reliable supply of domestic water to the settlement to which came from time to time remnants of clans from the Santa Rosa villages. There were a number of family dwellings in this village and it boasted two ceremonial houses.

Three Cahuilla clans lived at a site north of Agua Dulce where a very satisfactory well had been developed.

These three clans were more or less under the control of the clan whose Net had the one ceremonial house there. Within a radius of a few miles of this village there were other small communities one of which had a name which meant "Earth Crack."

Two clans of Desert Cahuilla resided at La Mesa. The larger of these clans comprised six families who shared one large communal house. A clan that once had lived at Indian Wells abandoned its lands there and moved in with the La Mesa people—thus further complicating the picture of aboriginal Cahuilla society.

The Desert Cahuilla village at Torres was dominated by two clans, and each of their Nets owned ceremonial houses there.

East and northeast of Mecca there were three small villages.

The literature on the subject does not mention the large village in the mesquite dunes along Pushawalla Wash out of the Indio Hills. In area, if not in the number of dwellings, it was at least as large as the Indian Wells village. Although it has not yet been positively identified as a Cahuilla site, there is every reason to believe that it was.

At a site about five miles northeast of Mecca, on the eastern side of the desert, at the entrance to Painted Canyon, there were twelve houses lived in by one clan. This was the clan to which Cabazon belonged. The village was called *Maswuut Helaat*, which means "The Place Where The Ceremonial Mats Are Spread." The name has real significance, for Cabazon was for many

50

years the spokesman, leader, and ceremonial Net for many of the Cahuilla villages in that area.

Francisco Nombre of the Desert Cahuilla group claimed that the Mexican authorities then in power in California granted papers to Cabazon giving him control over all the Cahuilla and Serrano Indians of the desert and over all native peoples from San Gorgonio Pass to Los Angeles!

This seems a rather large order, but we do know that, in addition to his own village in Painted Canyon, Cabazon was ceremonial leader for at least three other villages. One of these was located about three miles east of Thermal at the foot of the Indio-Mecca Hills. Another was midway between Mecca and Thermal, just east of the Southern Pacific Railroad. Still another village was that of *Palaiyil,* a very small one about three miles northeast of Thermal.

The Desert Cahuilla villages which were united under Cabazon may well have been the beginnings of a genuine tribal organization. When Cabazon died his son succeeded him as "chief," but by that time the inroads of the white man's civilization were taking their toll. The unity that might have made the Desert Cahuilla a vital force in southern California never was achieved.

CAHUILLA FOOD GATHERING

IF BY SOME POTENT MAGIC ONE could be transported in time and space to a ridge high above a Cahuilla Indian village of a century ago, and from that vantage point could observe the daily life of the village, we are sure that he would be impressed, first of all, by the stillness of the scene below him.

Many travelers to Cahuilla country have remarked on the virtual silence that seemed to envelop their villages.

David Prescott Barrows, in his invaluable study wrote: "There is a strange quietness surrounding these homes. . . . No loud voices are heard; the ordinary work of the household goes forward awaking but little sound. . . . A strange and somber loneliness hangs over an Indian village, especially at nightfall."

As one continued his observation of the village he would very soon realize that the primary concern of the people was the search for food.

Starvation was a constant threat to the Cahuilla, as it was to most of the Indian tribes of the arid Southwest. But it was a source of considerable astonishment to the first whites who came in contact with the Cahuilla that they were so well fed, living, as they did, in an environment that to the average white man would seem barren and sterile. The ability of the Cahuilla to find sufficient nourishment to survive in such a seemingly hostile region was due entirely to their thorough knowledge of the plants and animals in their territory that were suitable for food.

The women of the tribe were responsible for gathering all plant food. Even granting that the absence of food in the deserts and the mountains of southern California is more apparent than real, one is forced to admire the intelligence and ingenuity of these Cahuilla women in making possible for their people a more abundant food supply, and one of greater variety, than most tribes managed to have. The Cahuilla women were unusually apt in discovering ways and means of utilizing to the fullest possible extent, by leaching, soaking, grinding, and cooking, many plant products that to most of us would seem impossible as sources of nourishment.

Much of the daily life of Cahuilla women and girls was devoted to the collecting of plant food, especially seeds. They were very dexterous in extracting from even the smallest of plants the seeds they knew to be edible. This was done with a fan somewhat similar to a small tennis racquet. The seeds were "fanned" into a small, flat, tightly woven gathering basket placed firmly on the ground under the plant. When a sufficient quantity had been collected they were poured into a large packing basket.

A Cahuilla woman carried this packing basket in a net slung over her back with a carrying strap across her forehead, which was protected by a tight basket cap. This tumpline carrying device made it possible for both women and men to carry extremely heavy loads. Barrows speaks of an old woman who carried with apparent ease a stone mortar weighing one hundred fifty pounds!

The basic plant foods of all the Cahuilla—Western, Mountain, and Desert—were the mesquite beans of the desert and the acorns of the various oaks that grew in the mountains. One cannot help but feel that acorns and mesquite beans were twin staves of life to the Cahuilla.

The seed pod and the seeds of both species of mesquite, the "honey mesquite" and the "screw bean," were gathered in mid-summer. Everyone in the village joined in this important harvest. Then the pods were well dried and stored in great basket granaries. When needed for food both pods and seeds were pounded into a coarse meal, preferably in wooden mortars made from mesquite wood. This meal was then soaked in pottery bowls. Slight fermentation soon set in and this was thought to improve the flavor.

Mesquite pods are decidedly rich in nutrients, about twenty-five percent being a plant sugar. When one considers this and also is aware of how widespread the two species of mesquite are, he cannot help but speculate that those pioneer parties, which lost so many of their numbers by starvation in the deserts of California, could have profited by even a limited knowledge of Cahuilla food plants. Very possibly Death Valley in that case would never have been so named!

In autumn whole families moved up into the mountains to gather acorns. Sometimes the acorns were carried home to be stored in basket granaries. Sometimes they were pounded into a coarse meal while the family lingered at some favorite camping spot. Throughout the San Jacintos there can still be found the mortars which were worn into the bedrock on these annual treks.

Beside every Cahuilla dwelling one could see a shallow osier basket three or more feet in diameter. This was used in leaching out the tannic acid from the acorn meal. It would be partly filled with a carefully selected sand and placed on a low platform. The coarsely ground meal was patted down into a bowl-like depression in the sand and water was slowly poured over the meal until the leaching process was completed.

When this meal was to be used as food it was ground finer. This was done in a round stone mortar fitted with a basket hopper on top. A few handfuls of the coarse meal were placed in the mortar, often with a small quantity of

coarse iron pyrites, and pounded almost to a powder with a heavy, blunt-ended pestle about ten inches long. The meal was finally sifted and the iron pyrites and any coarse particles remaining were removed.

It has been said that the amount of sand, pieces of rock, and bits of iron pyrites in such meal was responsible for many of the Indians having teeth worn right down to the gums. However, Barrows states that during his work with the Cahuilla he often ate their food and he found it quite free from sand or grit of any kind.

Besides such staples as acorns, mesquite beans, and plant seeds, Cahuilla women harvested the fruits of many species of cacti, the small fruits of the native palm, and two species of wild plum. Every spring the new stalks and the cabbage-like heads of the agave were roasted in stone-lined pits. Strips and chunks of these roasted agaves would keep for long periods of time. They contained a great deal of a highly nutritious molasses-like substance. Even the yellow flowers of the agave were boiled and dried for future use.

The large seed pods of the Mohave yucca were roasted when they were green and were eaten uncooked when they were ripe. The flower stalks of other species of yucca and also of the yucca-like nolina were cut in chunks before they bloomed and roasted in fire pits over night. Their flowers, too, were boiled in pottery jars and used for food.

These are but a few of the almost endless list of desert and mountain plants which kept the Cahuilla relatively well fed.

While the women and girls were busy searching for and preparing plant foods, the men and the boys were busy contributing to the family larder. They were the hunters.

Community rabbit hunts were held frequently. Cahuilla men and boys, armed with bows and arrows and throwing sticks, would circle out though the desert, and they usually returned with dozens of cottontails and jack rabbits.

The bows used were from three-and-a-half to four-and-a-half feet long, and they were made of mesquite or of the so-called desert willow. Some of the arrows were made from the jointed reeds commonly found around springs and seeps. They were tipped with points of mesquite or of some other hard wood still further hardened by fire. Other arrows were made from a species of artemisia and from arrow-weed. These arrows were generally fitted with flaked points of various kinds of rocks.

Two types of throwing sticks were used by the Cahuilla. One was very similar to the boomerang-like rabbit stick of the Hopi. The other, which seems to have been the one in more common use, was a club-like implement, often made from the root or the branch of the red shank or ribbonwood.

On community hunts for rabbits or other small game, boys and unmarried young men did not take their game home. Instead they gave it to some family other than their own. It was thought that if an unmarried hunter were to eat the game he had killed he would inevitably die. When a young man planned to marry he began to supply game to the parents of the girl involved. There were many complex rules to be followed as to which individuals could eat the meat brought in by the tribal hunters and as to when it could be eaten.

Indeed many of these traditional taboos were observed right down to recent times. One old Cahuilla assured the writer that much of the illness among his people today is because they do not give proper consideration to the taboos concerned with animal food.

Elaborate ceremonial rites were involved in the hunting of large animals. Four of the largest animals were considered by the Cahuilla as sacred relatives: the grizzly bear, the jaguar—both of which are now extinct in California, the mountain lion, and the coyote. The grizzly bear was referred to as "great, great grandfather." When a Cahuilla came upon one he spoke to it with the greatest respect and urged it to go back into the distant mountains and hide so that it would come to no harm.

William Duncan Strong, in his *Aboriginal Society in Southern California,* tells of how a small party of Cahuilla came upon a female grizzly and her two cubs near where Beaumont is today. An old man in the party spoke to the bear quietly, explaining to her that they meant no harm so she should not bother them. Without further ado the three animals went peacefully away.

Only when a grizzly became a man killer did the Cahuilla get rid of it. Even then they tried to drive it away rather than to kill it. Shortly before the incident recounted by Strong, a party of Palm Springs Indians killed a grizzly which had killed two Mountain Cahuilla men. Afterward the Indians sang and danced around the body of the bear all night long.

When a man killed a deer he took it to the house of the clan Net, the ceremonial leader of the clan. If there had been no death in the clan of the hunter the people of his clan would assemble and hold a ceremonial sing throughout the night. In the morning the deer would be prepared for a clan feast. If there had been a death in the hunter's clan and this was the first deer slain after the death the Net would present the deer to the clan living nearest to him. The people of that clan would then have an all-night sing preliminary to the following day's feast. The first deer killed by a boy or a young man always went to his mother's clan.

When a young hunter killed a coyote or a bobcat he left it where it fell and returned to his village. There he told the news of his kill to such very old people as were well enough to safely use the meat and they would go get the animal. Many old people made a practice of following jaguar and mountain lion trails so as to profit by any meat killed by these animals. Thus their totemic animals granted them some slight measure of social security!

As hunting territory became more and more restricted with the influx of white settlers into Cahuilla territory, and as large animals became more and more scarce, the men were forced by dietetic demands to the hunting of smaller and smaller animals. With both the grizzly and the black bear* exterminated from the San Jacintos and

---

*Some scientists doubt that black bears were to be found in the San Bernardino and San Jacinto Mountains. Many informants among the Cahuilla assured the author that their fathers and grandfathers had seen black bears as well as grizzly bears in the San Jacintos. Joe Toutain, the well-known old-timer of Banning, tells us that he helped kill and eat a cinnamon bear (a color phase of the black bear) at Holcomb Flats in the San Bernardinos sometime between 1895 and 1900.

60

the Santa Rosas, with the herds of bighorn sheep decimated, with even the deer driven into the more remote foothill and mountain regions, the Cahuilla learned to use the meat of every small animal and large reptile that they could find. Naturally, too, their bows and arrows became smaller and more limited in power and craftsmanship as their animal targets deteriorated.

Although hunting and its intricate ceremonial customs largely filled the man's day and the collecting of plant food and its preparation left relatively few hours free to the women, there was much accomplished in other fields of endeavor. Ceremonial leaders might be found far and wide in the desert and in the mountains searching out the many and various plants required for both medicinal and ceremonial purposes. Women, particularly old women, were always busy making baskets.

Cahuilla baskets were of the coiled type. The core of the coil was grass, and around this were wrapped thin narrow strips of wood, sometimes from a sumac, frequently from the tough stalks of various rushes (wire grass). The basket maker kept a supply of these, cut to the proper length, by her side and deftly split them with her teeth as she needed them. The stems of these rushes varied in color throughout their length, from a dark red at the base to a light yellow brown at the top. These natural colors were supplemented by a series of vegetable dyes made from elderberries, from a small desert species of sea blite, and from one or more species of indigo bush. But one tool was needed in basket making, an awl, and this was usually made by setting a heavy cactus thorn or a sharp piece of bone in a wooden handle. In time a sharpened nail replaced the thorn or bone.

The designs in Cahuilla baskets were intricate and varied but their makers used no patterns. They held the designs accurately in mind until the basket was completed. They made their utility baskets water-tight by coating the inside of them with pitch or asphaltum. Small bits of either of these materials were placed in the basket together with hot stones. As the basket was rotated a layer of the melted material spread over it evenly.

In addition to baskets the Cahuilla made a number of other things from vegetable fibers. Their saddle mats, like those of their neighbors the Cupeño, were in great demand during the early American period in California. These "cocas" were woven on a small crude loom from the fibers of the Mohave yucca, and were about two-and-a-half by three feet in size.

The leaves of the Mohave yucca, so common in Cahuilla country, were soaked until the thick skin and the fleshy part were washed away. Then the fibers were buried in mud so as to whiten them. When ready for use they were combed out and some of them were dyed with various native dyes. Very tough sandals and different mats for household use were woven from them, as well as the popular saddle mats.

Fine cordage was made from the long tough fibers of the jointed reed found so commonly in wet places throughout the desert. From these fibers and also from those of the agave were made the carrying nets referred to earlier and the hammock cradles for Cahuilla babies.

Some coarse weaving was done with the native palm fibers. The stems of palm fronds were carved into stirring sticks and similar implements. The roots of the Mohave yucca and one of the pigweeds were ground up and used for soap.

Pottery making was another occupation of the Cahuilla women. Their method of making ollas, bowls, and dishes was somewhat similar to that of the Hopi and Pueblo pottery makers of Arizona and New Mexico. The clay was rolled out into long round "strings" and the vessel was built up by coiling these strings. The Cahuilla potter blended the coils and shaped the vessel by holding against the inside wall of it a specially made pottery disk or a smooth stone while she patted the outside of it with a wooden paddle. Many artists consider some Cahuilla ollas as graceful in form as those of the most famous of early European cultures.

The Cahuilla pottery makers made no attempt to keep the burning fuel, usually well dried dung, from touching the sides of the vessels. Thus the surface of their pottery was mottled black and brown. The Western Cahuilla, and possibly the two other branches of the tribe as well, sometimes decorated their jars with simple designs of dots and lines. These were painted on with some kind of mineral earth before firing.

Children and adults both played a variety of games similar to those played by other southwestern tribes. One very popular game was played by two teams of two men, or two boys, each. Each pair had a hard wooden ball about the size of a tennis ball. From a starting point this ball was kicked, barefoot, a mile or more and then back to the start. The team which got its ball back first, of course, was the winner.

Several gambling games also were played. One called *tepanish,* in Spanish *peon,* was played with small colored sticks during the annual mourning ceremonies. Both this game and "cat's cradle" had traditional and ceremonial significance. Although the makng of cat's cradles seems to be one of the most universal diversions of mankind, the Cahuilla have developed it to a point of exceptional complexity, the remembering of many complicated patterns being a requirement for entrance to the spirit world.

According to Mrs. Victoria Weirick, a member of the Wanikiktum clan of the Western Cahuilla, there was even a cat's cradle way to foretell the sex of an unborn infant. An elderly women friend of the child-bearing woman, when consulted as to the possible sex of the child, would make a rather simple cat's cradle pattern which, when the strings were finally pulled taut, might come out in one of two forms. If one of the two possible patterns came out three times in a row the child would be a boy. If the second possible pattern came out three times running, the child would, of course, be a girl.

It greatly amused Mrs. Weirick to demonstrate to us this unique prophetic device. Once when she pulled the strings taut and the pattern failed to come out properly I muttered, "Evidently a miscarriage!" She chuckled and tried again. All the time I was trying to photograph her efforts she talked away merrily, her remarks often being witty, and sometimes decidedly salty.

One curious feature of Cahuilla village life was the intricate system of gay and grave relationships which tradition had established. Every individual had to know the complex list of relatives with whom he was supposed to communicate with great solemnity. He had an equally long list of kin with whom he was expected to joke almost constantly.

A form of raillery in song was also commonly practiced by the Cahuilla. For example, one of the Coyote people might sing to the children of the Wildcat people a song, which in English goes, roughly like this.

> Wildcat with his arrows in his quiver does not
> look at all good to us.
> Coyote, brave Coyote, with his arrows in *his*
> quiver, looks very good to us.

These lines would be sung over and over again, always good-naturedly, but always teasingly.

The scene of greatest animation in or near any Cahuilla village—at any time of day and at any time during the year—was the village bathing pool. The Cahuilla seem to have had a passion for bathing. When the moon was in a certain position, first the girls and young women, and later the boys and young men would dash, at the first hint of dawn, to plunge into the pool while the reflection of the moon was still on the surface of the water. When there was a new moon the first boy to see it would call out to the other boys of the village and there would be another race to the pool and another swim—for good luck.

The pools usually had their source in the warm springs scattered here and there throughout Cahuilla-land and so afforded comfortable bathing and washing even during the cold days of winter.

Important activities, too, in every Cahuilla village included the use of the sweat lodge, meetings of the clan leaders in their special meeting houses, the daily care of small farm plots of corn, melons, beans, and squash—in villages fortunate enough to have water for irrigation purposes, the instruction of the boys and girls in the traditions of the tribe.

The observer on his over-looking ridge might well be impressed by the work and responsibility that fell to each member of a Cahuilla community ere the day was over.

As the tiny fires flickered in the night breeze old men would tell their tales of Cahuilla yesterdays, and the children would fall asleep to dream of *Mukat* and *Tamaiot*, the twin gods of Cahuilla creation, of the tiny clown *To* who danced on the head of the rattlesnake and of the beautiful moon goddess who had taught the tribe so many of its games.

To the folklore of the American Indian the Cahuilla Indians have contributed legends that are second to none in poetic content and in richness and breadth of imagination.

The tales which follow have been selected for retelling because they are the ones upon which many of the Cahuilla ceremonials are based. Needless to say, they vary in detail among the different Cahuilla groups—and according to the memory and the story-telling ability of the informant.

The versions used here have their origin in William Duncan Strong's *Aboriginal Society in Southern California* and Lucile Hooper's *The Cahuilla Indians*. This material has been supplemented by accounts the writer has been able to obtain from present-day Desert and Mountain Cahuilla.

CREATION MYTH

Before the beginnings of all things there was nothing but a mystic darkness, a darkness different from anything now known. This deeper-than-night darkness was permeated with strange, beautiful, far-away sounds—sounds such as might come from distant singers, but it was singing unlike that from the throat of man or bird. At times, these sounds were almost drowned out by eerie rumblings akin to muffled thunder.

Slowly this raven darkness divided into two even more formless masses, one male and one female. Suddenly colors appeared—red, white, blue, brown. These colors for a time flowed around each other, then seemed to intermingle. Finally they whirled into great male and female masses in such a way as to form one great sphere, a giant embryo that strove to conceive and to give birth.

Failure followed this first commingling and the colors whirled out from the masses, only to try a second time to become one with them. The second sphere failed, and again the colors whirled away.

When the colors and the masses flowed together for a third trial the monstrous ovule of creation was pierced

68

by vivid lightning-like flashes. Suddenly two embryos emerged, which grew very rapidly and soon were adult and able to speak.

These were the twin creators of the world—Tamaiot and Mukat.

For some time the two lay quietly, listening to the distantly-echoing sounds from their mother-darkness. At last Tamaiot spoke.

"I am older than you, Mukat, for I was first to hear from the great darkness the voices of our parents."

To this Mukat made angry objection.

"You are wrong. I was the first to hear their voices. I am the older."

Like all brothers they continued to quarrel, but they came to no conclusion as to their seniority. Tamaiot finally tried to change the subject.

"What can we do to dispel this darkness?" he asked.

There was scorn in Mukat's reply.

"You say that you are older than I and yet you do not know how to dissipate the darkness! Take a pipe from your heart and I will take one from mine, then we shall smoke."

Thereupon Mukat drew forth from his heart a black pipe. Tamaiot followed his example and reached into his own heart, but the pipe he drew forth from it was white. Then each again reached into his heart. From his heart Mukat drew forth black tobacco, but the tobacco Tamaoit drew forth was white.

"But," protested Tamaoit, "how can we smoke our sacred pipes if we have nothing with which to light them?"

Mukat laughed. "And yet you still claim that you are older than I when you can not even make a light for your pipe? I shall produce light for us both!"

Thereupon he drew from his heart the sun. But the sun slipped from his fingers. Both made every effort to catch it, but it rolled away and eluded them.

Solemnly Mukat again reached into his heart. This time he brought forth the western light of sunset. Not to be outdone, Tamaoit again reached into his heart and brought forth the eastern light of dawn. In silence both lit their pipes and smoked, and the smoke drifted upward and formed clouds in the darkness.

After a time they again took up their quarrel over who was the first-born. They began to tease each other, to outwit each other. They would hold their pipes in various positions and make each other guess as to how they were being held. At this game Mukat was always the winner— he always guessed right.

"Now it must be clear to you that I am older than you," he declared to Tamaoit.

To this Tamaoit only replied with a question, "What shall we do next?"

"From our hearts we must take the center pole, the axis, of the world," said Mukat.

Both reached into their hearts. From his Mukat drew forth a black pole, and from his Tamaoit drew forth a white pole. These joined to make the world's great hub.

"Stand up, center of the world, heart of the world-that-is-to-be!" they cried in concert, but the great pole would not stand up.

So Mukat and Tamaoit reached once more into their hearts. Now they brought forth snakes which encircled the gigantic pole, but still Mukat and Tamaoit could not hold it steady.

Then the brothers drew from their hearts huge rocks and propped them against the axis of the world-to-be, but still it would not stand straight.

Only when they brought forth spiders from their hearts—black from Mukat's and white from Tamaoit's— was the pole held firm. The mighty webs spun by these fabulous creatures kept the heart-pole of the world-to-be securely in its place.

Then the brothers climbed this great axis, singing as they climbed, and calling to each other, "Mukat!" "Tamaoit!" "Tamaoit!" "Mukat!"

When they reached the top they sang out together, "We, Mukat and Tamaoit, are sitting on the very pinnacle of the world-that-is-to-be!"

For a time they sat looking down at the place from whence they had come. Tamaoit was the first to speak.

"What is that mass of smoke and cloud below?" he asked.

"That," said Mukat, "has come from our after-birth. Therein lie all the sicknesses which will befall man-that-is-to-be."

Mukat named over all these ills, and the brothers were sad as they thought of the suffering that man was to endure.

"But," said Mukat, "when the time comes we shall give power to certain ones so that they can cure these sicknesses. Certain men and certain women will be the doctors in the world-that-is-to-be."

"Let us make the directions now," said Tamaoit. "Which shall we make first?"

"As I am the older," said Mukat, "we shall name first the direction where I now am. It shall be West."

In turn then they named North, South, and finally East.

When this was done together they declaimed, "when man-that-is-to-be enters into his ceremonial house he must blow to the world directions in this order—West, North, South, East. Thus he will remember Mukat and Tamaoit and know that they created the world."

"Is it not time that we make the world?" asked Tamaoit. "How can we do it?"

"As I am the older," said Mukat, "I shall show you. Do as I do."

Mukat drew forth from his heart black earth which he placed on top of the world-to-be. Then Tamaoit drew forth from his heart white earth which he placed on top of the axis of the world-to-be. But the black earth and the white earth crumbled apart and were lost.

For the second time Mukat drew forth from his heart black spiders, and Tamaoit white spiders. The spiders spun great webs in all directions about the center pole of the world-to-be, and these webs held fast the black earth and the white earth which the brothers produced from their hearts in large quantities. Then from the hearts of Mukat and Tamaoit came ants of all kinds. These set busily to work to spread the black earth and the white. Thus was the world created.

Then Mukat and Tamaoit drew forth from their hearts two whirlwinds to help the ants distribute the earth, and from his heart Tamaoit produced a great ocean which he spread around the earth to help hold it in place. Then the brothers created all the animals and plants that belong in the ocean and many sacred things for use by the doctors and the ceremonial leaders of the people that were yet to be created.

Now from their hearts the twin creators brought forth the sky. The sky swayed and bent in the wind and Mukat and Tamaoit pondered as to how it could be held in place, against the great darkness from which they themselves had so recently been brought forth. For this purpose they decided to create stars to pin the sky above, and then they sent the two whirlwinds to the very edges of the earth there to hold the ends of the sky firmly in place.

All this done, Mukat and Tamaoit turned their attention to creating the creatures of the earth. Tamaoit created as first of all animals the coyote. Coyote was to be their assistant in distributing all over the world the other animals they were about to produce. Mukat then created the horned owl, whose ability to see in the dark was of great value to them.

With the animals created and distributed throughout the earth, Mukat and Tamaoit started to work on man. Each started to form a body, but Tamaoit worked too fast and the body he made was ugly and misshapen. The brothers worked long and hard and formed many bodies, and as each one was finished Coyote carried it to one side and Horned Owl cried, "Who-o-o!"

Mukat found working in the darkness too difficult, so he reached into his heart and brought forth *Man-el*, the Moon Maiden, a beautiful woman who shone with a bright white light. This light fell upon the ugly, misshapen forms which Tamaoit had made. Whereupon Mukat scolded him severely and the brothers quarreled violently.

"I shall go to the bottom of the earth," declared Tamaoit, "and I shall take all our creations with me!"

"Take with you your ugly, hideous creatures," said Mukat, "but you cannot take the forms I have created."

Then in great anger Tamaoit sang out the song which was his, and blew upon the earth. A great quake occurred. The earth opened up. Into the cavity disappeared Tamaoit and all his ugly creations.

With the closing of the fissure after him the mountains of the earth were formed. Mukat found that Tamaoit had even tried to take the sky with him and he had to wrestle with one of the fierce whirlwinds for its possession. Mukat won the great struggle, and the sky remained over the earth. One can still see five bright stars where the fingers of Mukat's hand pressed hard as he strove to hold the sky firmly in place.

At last the earth grew calm and quiet after the departure of Tamaoit. Then Mukat's forms began to move— life had come to them. But while Mukat was still struggling with the wind, all the white people stole away to the far north. Suddenly the sun, which earlier had eluded the brothers, reappeared. The people nearby were burned black by its rays, those farther off were only slightly browned, while the ones who had slipped away to the north were not affected at all.

Fear struck all the people and the animals with the coming of Sun, and they began to speak in a confusion of sounds. Mukat could not understand a word that was being said and he was greatly distressed by the babel of noise. He listened carefully to find a familiar sound and at last he heard one man speaking in Cahuilla, his own tongue.

Mukat singled this man out of all the chattering mass and named him the ancestor of all the Cahuilla people, and he now lives in the abode of the sun and the moon and the evening star. Thus the language spoken by the Cahuilla of today is the original language of all mankind.

MAN-EL, THE MOON MAIDEN

After Tamaoit left, Mukat and his people lived happily together in a great community house. Manel, the Moon Maiden, lived with them and she did many things that brought joy to all of them. Among the many games she taught them were complicated forms of "cat's cradle," the game that begins with looping strings on the fingers so as to form a sort of cradle. Man-el seemed to know an infinite number of ways to transfer the loops from finger to finger so as to make all kinds of intricate patterns.

One of Mukat's first actions was to create a place wherein the spirits of the dead could dwell. This place was in the East and was known as *Telmekish*. By pulling out one of his whiskers and pointing it toward the east he made a spirit road. At the end of this road there was a great gate, guarded by a man-spirit, *Monkatwet*, who never slept and never died.

Just beyond Monkatwet's gate there were two hills that were in constant movement, coming together and moving apart again and again and again. If an evil spirit tried to pass between these hills, the hills moved together and crushed it, whereupon the evil spirit was transformed into a rock, a bat, or a butterfly. If the spirit had lived a good life the moving hills would permit it to pass safely between them and journey on to Telmekish.

Mukat taught his people not to sleep with their heads toward the East for that was the direction death would take. This was not so important, however, when one was old and little life was left to him.

Man-el's cat's cradle game played a role in the journey of the spirit to Telmekish. Every person had to remember many complicated patterns and be able to demonstrate them to the guardian of Telmekish, Monkatwet, before he would permit the spirit to pass through the gates.

Every morning Man-el took Mukat's people and animals to the water, and they would spend the day there, swimming and playing happily together and learning the wonderful songs that Man-el taught them. The people were always ready to laugh, too, at one of their number, a tiny man called To who was most amusing when he danced or sang a song.

There was one animal that always stayed behind with Mukat when Man-el and the others went to the water. This was Rattlesnake, who remained coiled up beside Mukat's door. In those days Rattlesnake had neither teeth nor poison.

Every evening when the people and the animals returned to Mukat's big house To jumped on top of Rattlesnake's head and danced and sang. Although To was very tiny his constant dancing made Rattlesnake's head flatter and flatter. Finally Rattlesnake complained to Mukat. Mukat promptly pulled out two short whiskers to which he added poison before giving them to Rattlesnake for teeth.

"Now," said Mukat to Rattlesnake, "when To comes back and starts to dance upon your head you can bite him. But once you have bitten him you must leave my big house and hide among the rocks."

The next time little To danced upon Rattlesnake's head the reptile bit him and then followed Mukat's warning and hid among the rocks. Rattlesnake was the first animal to leave Mukat's house, and he never returned to it.

One day Mukat looked at Man-el and suddenly realized how beautiful she was. He decided to make her his wife. He did not tell her this at once, but Man-el sensed it and she knew that the time had come for her to leave. Sadly she went about performing certain duties before her departure. One day she taught the women how to use certain plants for medicines, and that night she disappeared. So that the people could not follow her, she ordered multitudes of ants and beetles to crawl back and forth over her tracks.

Early in the morning the people and the animals realized that Man-el, the Moon Maiden, was gone from among them and they were heartbroken. Coyote dashed down to the water. Seeing Moon's reflection in it he jumped in after her, but he could not find her. As soon as the waters had calmed, Coyote again jumped in to rescue her but again she disappeared. High in the sky Moon watched Coyote and when he came out of the water for the second time she called to him. He looked up and saw her, serene and beautiful, in the morning sky. He pleaded with her to return, but she only smiled.

Coyote returned to the big house and told the people what had happened. For many days they grieved over having lost their playmate and their teacher.

THE DEATH OF MUKAT

One of the many things that Mukat taught his people was how to make bows and arrows. He explained to them that they must choose the proper wood, and that it must be dried thoroughly. Then he taught them how to make arrow points. When the first lot of bows and arrows were finished the people laid them on the ground. From the arrows came a strange noise that frightened the people, but Mukat assured them that both the arrows and the bows were harmless.

Tahquitz, to whom Mukat had granted magic powers, held one of the arrows high above his head and said, "Why be afraid of this? Look!"

He jabbed the arrow right through his stomach, and the people marveled that it made no wound.

Then Mukat divided his people into two groups. These two bands began to run about and shoot arrows into each other as if it were a game. A great cloud of dust arose, and the people could not see what they were doing. When all their arrows were used up and the dust had settled, they were sad at finding that some of the people were dead and that they could not bring them back to life.

78

"Do not be concerned," said Mukat. "They will return."

The dead did return that night, but only as spirits, whereupon Mukat told them about the next world, Telmekish.

"This world," said he, "is a place where children are born. In Telmekish there is no sickness and no sorrow, and life there goes on forever."

Mukat had now done three things which caused the people to distrust him. He had driven away Man-el, the Moon Maiden. He had made Rattlesnake bite To and kill him. Now he had given the people bows and arrows to kill each other, and this after promising them that the bows and arrows were harmless. They felt that there was nothing for them to do but kill Mukat.

First the people asked Bear and Mountain Lion to kill him, but these two refused, saying that it would be better to have someone bewitch him.

The people never knew what Mukat did at night, for they always slept very soundly. They decided to ask the white lizard that can run away up into the mesquite trees to run to the top of the great house and keep watch all night. The white lizard saw Mukat light his pipe and blow magic smoke over the people to make them sleep. Then he left the big house and walked some distance away to defecate, and returned to the house.

The following night Frog hid by the spot where Mukat had gone the night before and, having power to bewitch, he used that power. Mukat realized that something was making him ill. He felt around with his cane and scratched Frog three times on his back. Even today you can see the three marks which he made.

Mukat returned to the house and asked the people to help cure him. Medicine men worked over him, but they did not even try to use their power to cure. As Mukat grew more and more ill he sent Swallow to North Wind with orders that North Wind come to help him. But North Wind only came and covered him with sand, so Mukat drove him away. Swallow brought the other winds, too, but they were of no avail in helping to make Mukat well.

Crow was sent to bring food to the sick man, but when Crow found the food he just ate and ate and never returned. Dove was sent to the mountains to bring back pine nuts. Mukat ate all of them, but he was still hungry. Then he asked Hawk to bring him some meat, but, like Crow, Hawk never returned.

By this time Mukat knew that his animal people were deserting him. Despondent, he asked the locusts to sing for him. As they sang he realized that he was about to die.

All the time that he had been ill Coyote had sat beside him, but now Mukat became afraid of Coyote. He asked the people to send Coyote to get fire to light his funeral pyre. Coyote was reluctant to go, but the people told him that, as the fastest runner, it was his duty to go.

Mukat then began to sing the sacred songs so that his soul would go to Telmekish, and as he sang he died.

All the animals with big claws helped dig a large pit for the body of Mukat. Mountain Quail and Desert Quail brought eleven different kinds of wood for the funeral pyre. Fly rotated a fire drill in dry palm wood and started the fire. That is why even today flies are always rubbing their hands as if they were spinning the fire drill.

The people formed a tight circle around the fire, and when Coyote returned he could not get through. Finally he jumped over the heads of the people and, dashing into the fire, he seized the heart of Mukat and ran off with it to the mountains.

Before Mukat died he had told the people that they should burn his big house and that once every year they should hold memorial services for the dead, of six nights' duration. He had shown them, too, how to make an effigy of each person who had died, and he had explained how they should dance with these images, so that the spirits of the dead would return and be with them for these six nights.

The people followed Mukat's directions and the very first ceremonial for the dead was the one they held for Mukat himself, with Coyote acting as Net.

When the memorial was at an end Raven returned to the place where Mukat's body had been burned and he fell into the pit and got himself all black, which is why ravens are so black today.

One day Buzzard saw some strange plants growing in the pit. As the people did not know what kind of plants they were they sent a man to question the spirit of Mukat.

"The people killed me before I had taught them about these plants," said the spirit of Mukat. "The tobacco is for old people to smoke for the comfort it will give them. The melons, pumpkins, and corn are good foods for all the people. Tell them to grow them and enjoy them."

Mukat had given Tahquitz the power to perform various supernatural acts, believing that Tahquitz would use his power to help the people. Tahquitz, however, had begun to use this power mischievously and lecherously. As he did more and more harm to mankind he became so feared and disliked that he had to leave the Cahuilla people.

His face black with anger at being driven forth, Tahquitz strode up the canyon that now bears his name. He climbed high and far into the San Jacinto Mountains and there, in a mysterious cave under a gigantic rock, he made his home. Many Cahuilla believe that this magic cave, with its walls of transparent rock, is located directly under the phallic symbol of Tahquitz Rock.

To this cave Tahquitz carried the souls of men and women whom he had lured from their people and captured to satisfy his gross appetites. Although no one could see into his cave, Tahquitz himself and all his prisoners could look out through the strange glassy walls and clearly see all that was going on in the world of man far below.

Like man-spirits of evil Tahquitz did most of his hunting by night, and he often can be seen as a giant meteor streaming across the sky. Many Cahuilla have seen him in the daytime as well—a gigantic, evil-looking old man, lurking in lonely places to await his next victim.

Once a beautiful Cahuilla girl of the Agua Caliente people was bathing all alone in a big clear pool in the lower end of Tahquitz Canyon. Tahquitz saw her and was entranced with her rare beauty. He determined at once that she was to be his wife.

Disregarding her pitiful pleas, he seized her and carried her rapidly up the canyon and over the mountain to his cave. There Tahquitz was kind to her and made his other captives act as servants to her. He presented to her the souls of many people, which he forced her to eat with him. The girl abhorred him, and she wept bitterly when he demanded that she share his victims with him.

The poor girl continued to be so very unhappy that after several years Tahquitz himself felt sorry for her and he told her that she could return to her home and to her people. But he made her promise that for three years she would tell no one where she had been or of her relations with him. If she broke her promise she would die immediately, he said. She gave her promise and thereupon Tahquitz led her safely down the mountain slopes and into Tahquitz Canyon, to the very pool where he had first discovered her.

The Agua Caliente people had lost all hope of seeing her again. When she walked into her village, alive and well, there was great rejoicing. They questioned her as to where she had been, but at their questions she only shook her head and said nothing.

As the months went by the constant questioning by her family, her friends, and the old leaders of the village made life unbearable for her. The more firmly she refused to answer them the more insistent they became. She could stand it no longer.

She told her people to build a large house and to assemble there and she would tell them her secret. The evening that the house was finished the whole village gathered there. The girl, knowing full well that to break her promise to Tahquitz meant instant death, stood before them with tears streaming down her face.

She told of how Tahquitz had surprised her at the bathing pool, of how he had carried her away and made her his wife, of the horrible life she had lived in the glass-rock cave high in the mountains, and of his ghastly appetite for the souls of men. When she told of how he had forced her to share his victims with him the people cried out in horror and shrank away from her. All alone she made her way to her house and fell upon her bed. In the morning she was dead, just as Tahquitz had prophesied.

Even today strange rumblings can be heard in the rocky depths of the San Jacintos, and earthquakes are common there. Without doubt these are caused by Tahquitz as he stamps about and throws great masses of rock at his unwitting victims deep in his mountain cave beneath Tahquitz Rock.

Tahquitz sometimes still appears to Cahuilla people as a huge ugly creature with an arrow stuck right through his massive head. Ambrosia, the old medicine man of the Desert Cahuilla, saw him often, and said he looked like any other Cahuilla man except for the evil which could be clearly discerned in his hideous face.

That evil is rampant even today. Many tragic accidents can be traced to him. Almost nightly in the midnight sky one can see a flaming meteor—old Tahquitz in search of the souls of men and women to sate his horrible appetite.

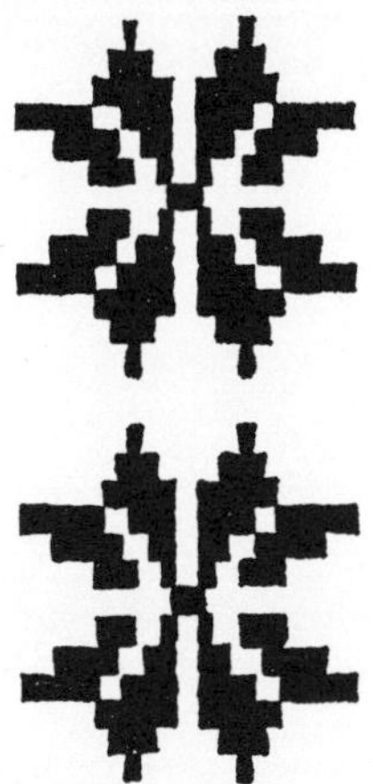

UNTIL ABOUT A CENTURY AGO
the ceremonial life of the Cahuilla Indians was a rich and
varied one. Again, it speaks well for the high level of Cahuilla intelligence that, despite the ceaseless struggle for
subsistence in their rugged environment, these Indians of
the windy San Gorgonio Pass, the arid deserts, and the
high mountains still could spare time for the involved and
lengthy ceremonies that marked every important stage

in the career of the individual and that embellished the community life of every village group. Birth, puberty, marriage, the naming of children, death, cremation, burial, food gathering, hunting—all these events and many more were solemnized with interesting rites.

Several years have passed since the death of the last of those old Indians who knew, first-hand, much about these Cahuilla ceremonies. That today we have any reliable account of them is due almost entirely to the pioneer work of such scientists as David Prescott Barrows, Lucile Hooper, A. L. Kroeber, and William Duncan Strong and to the observations of the Franciscan Father G. Boscana. It is to their publications and to a few informants among older Cahuilla still living that the author is indebted for the material in the accounts which follow.

Each Cahuilla village was such an independent entity that it is almost impossible to give a generalized account of even the simplest ceremony that could be considered truly accurate in its details so far as every village of the linguistic group was concerned.

To further complicate the ceremonial picture, there was born, prior to the appearance of the Spaniards in California, at the Indian village of *Pubuna*, near Los Alamitos, a religious leader called variously *Chinigchinich*, *Wiamot*, *Tobet*, etc. Chinigchinich founded a cult, the ceremonal observances of which spread throughout a number of southern California Indian tribes. There is proof that the Mountain Cahuilla adopted many of the aspects of this cult into their ceremonial life. There is considerable reason to believe that some of the Western

Cahuilla did so. It is still a matter of debate as to how much—if at all—the Desert Cahuilla were influenced by it.

THE CEREMONY FOR THE DEAD

In all Cahuilla communities the most important religious rite was the nearly week-long memorial ceremony performed annually for those who had died during the year. Among the Western Cahuilla in the San Gorgonio Pass area it was observed when the constellation of Orion—*Patem,* or bighorn sheep—was at the zenith; among other Cahuilla, sometime during the winter months. According to Cahuilla tradition, the Ceremony for the Dead was their oldest ceremony. It had been taught to them by Mukat himself.

The Ceremony for the Dead is still being observed by some of the Cahuilla groups, but to a limited extent, and in abbreviated form. On the Morongo Reservation those of Cahuilla blood join in such observance of the memorial as is carried on in the gaunt frame building near the Catholic church. The old school building close to the hot spring near present-day Anza is the site where what is left of the Mountain Cahuilla version of the ceremony is performed.

On the Torres-Martinez Reservation of the Desert Cahuilla Indian "Captain" William Levy maintained a ceremonial "big house," and he presided over the rituals there until his death in the summer of 1958. At that time, in accordance with custom, the ceremonial house, all the ceremonial paraphernalia, and Captain Levy's home were burned to the ground. Also on this reservation, at the end of a winding dirt road, not far from the old Indian Agency headquarters, Jesus ("Jess") Kintano still directs the annual ceremony in his well-built, well-maintained "big house" in a grove of giant tamarisks.

In the old days the Ceremony for the Dead was presided over by the Net, the religious leader of the clan holding the ceremony. He had two assistants, the *Paha* and the *Takwa*. Paha was in charge of the singing, and it was he who signaled the beginning of each act of the rite. The Takwa was responsible for the gathering of food for the ceremony and for its later distribution. There were also many medicine men who performed acts of magic of a sleight-of-hand nature. These men were also thought to have supernatural powers, and some of them were greatly feared by their fellow tribesmen.

Many months before the ceremony, the Net would hold a council with the old men of his clan to decide which individuals of other communities would be invited to participate. One man of this group would be appointed to make a personal call upon each one selected and officially invite him to be present. Acceptance of the invitation was indicated by the presentation to the messenger of money or other gifts. If the person invited was the ceremonial leader of his clan, his gift to the messenger was a long string of shell money. It was expected that these presents would be returned in similar manner when the clans of the donors held their own ceremonials for the dead.

On the day before the ceremony a community rabbit hunt was held by the men and boys of the village to provide plenty of jackrabbits and cottontails for a huge rabbit stew. Long tables were set up in the ceremonial house and a cooking fire was started, for there the guests would be fed throughout the week.

Chief among the preparations for the ceremony were those made by close relatives of the deceased for whom the rites were to be held. Life-sized effigies of the dead were made out of cloth stuffed with grass, with wigs of human hair, and buttons or coins for eyes. Each effigy was suitably, often elaborately, clothed.

The Ceremony for the Dead required six full nights, and most of it took place within the kishumnawat, or ceremonial house. On the day before it began the Net would appoint a man to greet the participants invited from other villages. This man, wearing only a breech clout, watched the trails and roads carefully. Upon sighting the arrivals he ran throughout the village, announcing that the guests were in sight. Then the whole village ran out, and certain men and boys shot arrows into the air. Upon their arrival the guests would be escorted to the house where they would live during the week, then they would assemble at the ceremonial house, where the Paha took them to their proper places on the seats that had been placed around the wall.

Once the guests were seated the Net would go to each one in turn, kneel before him, and welcome him, presenting a package of tobacco as he did so. Each guest then would give the Net a small gift, usually of shell or other money, wrapped up in a handkerchief. After this official welcome the Paha would invite all the guests to feast upon the food which had been prepared for them, usually rabbit stew, bread, and coffee. This meal was a solemn one and there was little talking during it.

At night villagers and guests assembled around the fire in the kishumnawat for the beginning of the rites. The first three nights were devoted to retelling the Cahuilla creation myth. This took the form of chants in a peculiar minor key, and was led by the Paha. At intervals the singers would stop and the Paha would utter strange grunting sounds, throw back his head, and blow straight up into the air. The singers would imitate his actions before again taking up the chant.

During these first three nights the proceedings would be enlivened by acts of magic performed by the medicine men. Even as recently as 1918, Casimiro, a famous Desert Cahuilla medicine man, put on an especially novel act. With surprising speed he jumped up from his place and tied around his head a band into which he put three bundles of owl feathers. Then, picking up a round wooden wand about eight inches long tipped with owl feathers, he began to shuffle about the fire, all the time singing and jumping up and down. Suddenly he began to shake. The shaking became of such intensity that he could hardly stand. At this point he thrust the wooden wand down his throat two or three times. On the third time he brought up some small object—"out from his heart"—and the violent shaking ceased.

Casimiro, like many other Cahuilla medicine men, was also a fire-eater. He would take from the fire a glowing ember about the size of an egg and place it in his mouth. Holding it there long enough for his audience to see the red glow inside his mouth, he would then inhale through his nostrils and blow sparks out from his mouth. Finally he would crush the now cold ember between his teeth and spit it out. Sometimes he would repeat this performance several times a night.

During the first three nights the young men present often participated in dances appropriate to the ceremony, and during the final three nights the guests were permitted to sing their ceremonial songs. As these performances continued throughout the night the children —and some of the adults, too—would fall asleep and stretch out on the floor, to wake from time to time and join in the songs.

The climax of the ceremonial was reserved for the end of the sixth night. Just before sunrise the Net would lead into the kishumnawat a procession of women, walking two by two and carrying the effigies of their dead. The woman carrying the effigy was always a close relative of the deceased. This procession circled the interior of the ceremonial house and all the other participants joined it, chanting a low song of mourning and occasionally punctuating the chant with a wailing cry.

The Net then would lead the procession outside the kishumnawat into the brush enclosure that surrounded it. There the women with the effigies would form a circle and begin a dance. In the dance they would draw themselves up on their toes, then bend forward and come down hard on their heels. As this dance ended the members of the clan holding the ceremony would throw money and bits of cloth on the images as their tokens of respect for the dead. Members of the officiating clan could not touch these items, but outsiders were not prohibited from doing so, and the money especially sometimes disappeared quickly.

At this point the women carrying the images would march in a single file to the graveyard. There the images were burned.* No one save the women themselves was permitted to view this solemn phase of the ceremony.

While these women were engaged in this final act, the Net would make the rounds of the guests and hand them long strings of ceremonial shell money. These the guests were to keep until their own clan memorials were held. With this gesture of the Net the Ceremony for the Dead came to a close.

During the time when the older people were preoccupied with the formal rites of the week, the younger people usually played the gambling game known as tepanish. It is believed that this game once had some religious significance, but if so it has been lost entirely.

As the ceremonial life of the Cahuilla gradually eroded away, the Ceremony for the Dead became the one ceremonial of the year and with it were performed some of the rites originally part of other religious observances. With the passing of time the deep religious significance of the ceremony has practically disappeared and today is treasured chiefly in the failing memories of the ever-decreasing number of old Cahuilla men and women.

THE INITIATION RITES FOR GIRLS AND BOYS

The girls of a Cahuilla community were initiated into womanhood with an involved purification rite. A large pit was dug in the center of the ceremonial house and a

---

*Some Cahuilla groups burned the images at a spot close to the ceremonial house.

fire built in it. When the ground was thoroughly heated
the fire was scraped out and the depression lined with
grass. The girls were then laid on this carpet of grass and
covered with more grass and hot sand. This was done for
three nights—in the daytime the girls were kept at home.
At intervals during the night the girls were removed
from the pit long enough to reheat it.

During these nights the old men and the old women
danced around the girls in the pits, singing songs which,
according to Cahuilla tradition, had been taught them
by the goddess of the moon when she lived among the
Cahuilla.

During the three days of the ceremony the only food
permitted to the initiates was a bitter tea prepared by the
old women, and even after the ceremony was at an end
the girls were expected to adhere to a number of taboos.
They could not eat meat, salt, or fruit. They could not
scratch their heads with their fingers, but must use scratch-
ing sticks. They could not drink or wash in cold water.

No doubt some phases of this initiation ceremony have
been completely forgotten, for it has not been performed
for a long time. In the territory of both the Mountain and
the Western Cahuilla angular, diamond-shaped paintings
have been found on rocks, paintings similar to those used
in the adolescent rites of Luiseño Indian girls.

Mr. Glenn Payne of Cabazon directed the writer to one
such pictograph high in the San Jacintos. The unique
rock sculpturing of this area would certainly have made
it a natural and impressive site for initiation rites. A very
curious small cave near the pictograph bears evidence of
its having been used ceremonially. Unhappily, we have

been unable to secure from our informants any sign of recognition of the site or of the meaning of the pictograph.

* * * *

Initiation rites for the boys were held every few years among the Mountain Cahuilla, and possibly among some groups of the Western Cahuilla. The ceremony was known as the *Manet* ceremony, and it was closely allied to the ceremonies prescribed by the Chinigchinich cult referred to earlier.

Several days before the time set for the ceremony the older people of the community met to determine which boys were ready for initiation. Then the boys were taught by their fathers the songs of their clan and also the "enemy" songs of other clans or even of other tribes. The teaching of these songs was supervised by the Paha. The Paha also prepared strings of eagle and red-shafted flicker feathers to be used in the dances which formed part of the ceremony. The Net appointed one man to act as instructor of the boys in the dances and as their leader when the dances were performed. This man always took the initiates to some secluded place for the practice that was necessary for both the dances and the songs involved in the ceremony.

Mr. Otho W. Moore of Indio, as a boy in the early 1900's, was very well acquainted with the Indians in the Torres-Martinez area of the desert, and he knew Ambrosia, a Desert Cahuilla medicine man of that day. Ambrosia once told him of taking a group of young men to a ceremonial place somewhere in the Santa Rosa-San Jacinto mountain region where they spent several months so that Ambrosia could thoroughly indoctrinate them in tribal ceremonial lore.

The dances learned by the boys were performed by them at night in the ceremonial house. This part of the ceremony was more or less a public affair. During the dances relatives of the boys threw baskets and other gifts among them. Any guests present were privileged to gather in these gifts.

The rites which followed these dances were secret and could be participated in or observed only by the older men of the clan and by those young men who had already been initiated. These secret rites seem to have been added as a result of the Chinigchinich influence. They were performed within the ceremonial house, and those not qualified to be present were warned away by the leader whirling a bull-roarer. (The bull-roarer is a thin wooden paddle on a long string and it has been used in primitive rites since ancient times.)

For these rites the Net prepared *toloache,* a narcotic drink made from datura (Jimson weed). He carefully ground up the dried weed, using a special mortar and pestle for the purpose. Then he added water to the finely ground powder and poured the concoction into a red pottery bowl. The Paha passed the bowl of toloache to each boy, who was expected to drink at least a small quantity of it.

After every boy had drunk of the toloache the dancing was resumed. For this part of the ceremony the boys were naked. One by one the men present each seized a boy by the waist and danced with him several times around the central fire. So powerful are the narcotic properties of Jimson weed that many of the boys fell unconscious, and sometimes, it is said, a boy died. The toloache was supposed to produce visions similar to those experienced by the tribal medicine men, and things seen in these visions were looked upon as having deep religious significance for the initiates.

The toloache drinking took place on only the first evening of the secret rites, but the dancing was kept up every night for a week. The whole ceremony ended with the Net making a symbolic design in a shallow saucer-like depression in the ground. At one such ceremony in the old village of Cahuilla the Net drew a design like the spokes of a wheel, using for the design colors derived from brownish-red iron oxide, from a black mineral-like substance, and from ground-up white clay.

The Mountain Cahuilla subjected the boys to one further ordeal. The initiates were led to places where large red ants had nested. Here shallow pits were dug. Then each boy was given a long whisk of nettles to brush off the fiercely biting ants and he was rolled into the pit. This painful experience was supposed to develop within its victim great bravery and endurance as a hunter.

We have found no evidence that the rites of the Chinigchinich cult extended into the villages of the Desert Cahuilla. The initiation rites for boys in these villages probably were of a much simpler nature.

THE FIRE DANCE

On the concluding night of the Manet ceremony for the boys some Cahuilla clans staged a spectacular Fire Dance.

96

A great fire was built outside the ceremonial house. Around this fire men and women of the clan circled in a sort of dance, chanting songs appropriate to the occasion. At one point during the evening the dancing suddenly became faster and faster and at its climax the men, with sharply defined movements, sat down in a circle around the fire. The women and children stood behind them, continuing to chant.

With their bare feet the men began to push the fire in toward the center. Occasionally a man fainted from the heat and fell back unconscious, whereupon a medicine man, using a sheaf of feathers, fanned him back to consciousness.

At a certain signal the men shifted their positions, and this time they used their bare hands to force the coals toward the center of the fire! Some informants claimed that as the excitement mounted, the medicine men sometimes jumped right into the fire and danced on the red embers until the fire was danced out.

Why the participants in this spectacular Fire Dance—and the fire-eaters in the Ceremony for the Dead—suffered no injury of any kind remains a mystery to this day.

THE EAGLE DANCE

The Eagle Dance was a very popular ceremony among the Mountain Cahuilla especially. It could be performed at any time, but in later years it frequently followed the Ceremony for the Dead.

The beginning of the Eagle Dance was announced by a leader who whirled a bull-roarer around and around over his head as he called to the people to assemble in a

EAGLE DANCER

circle in front of the ceremonial house. To attract those who did not respond to his summons promptly, he engaged in all sorts of clownish antics. Meantime the men who were to participate in the dance gathered within the ceremonial house, and a man with a long pole was stationed in the doorway to keep any onlookers from crowding around the entrance.

The dancers were naked except for kilts and head-dresses of eagle feathers—or, occasionally in the old days, of condor feathers. Each dancer's face was painted with white clay, and he carried two short, roughly carved sticks.

When all was ready and the people had assembled, the leader of the dance stared up at the sun for several minutes in utter silence. Then the silence was sharply broken by the first dancer dashing out of the ceremonial house. He ran to the circle of observers and knelt down, and he, too, stared in silence at the sun. Then suddenly he hit his sticks together as a signal for the people to begin to sing. As they sang he slowly moved about within the circle, imitating the movements of the eagle or the condor. At another signal from his sticks the audience surrounding him sang faster and faster, and some of them even joined in the dance.

Then the dancer began to whirl. Soon he was spinning so fast that his feather kilt flew out at right angles to his waist. At a shout from the leader the door-keeper cleared everyone from the entrance to the ceremonial house. The dancer stopped his whirling and dashed back into the house as abruptly as he had appeared from it. In turn each participant went through this amazing performance.

This whirling dance also seems to have stemmed from the Chinigchinich cult, but to all Cahuilla the eagle and the condor were closely associated with the sun and, therefore, they granted great reverence to these monarchs of the California sky. Anyone who has been privileged to watch the effortless, gliding flight of these noble birds high above even our highest mountain summits can well understand why they were revered so highly.

It is hoped these very brief descriptions of a very limited number of the ceremonies of the Cahuilla Indians will give the reader some conception of the richness and variety of their ritual life. Fortunately many of the songs that were such an important part of the ceremonies have been recorded by competent anthropologists. Who knows but maybe the day will come when young Cahuilla will journey to Berkeley and to Los Angeles to listen to and to learn from those recorded echoes of Cahuilla yesterdays?

VII

Of the individual Cahuilla Indians whose names appear on the pages of history the ones who have most captured the imagination of the white man are Fig Tree John, Juan Antonio, Ramona and Alessandro. The last two, their names always paired, are no doubt the best known, and yet in a sense they never really existed. They were fictional characters engendered in the fertile brain of Helen Hunt Jackson to become the heroine and hero of her novel *Ramona*.

Their story is told anew every spring in the Ramona Outdoor Play presented in the Ramona Bowl by the people of Hemet and San Jacinto. This "pageant," as it is popularly known, is one of the most successful of the outdoor events staged in the Southwest. Those of us who like some semblance of authenticity in such things may be a bit disturbed by its young Indian dancers garbed in Plains Indian war bonnets, but, nevertheless, it is a mighty good show, performed in a splendid setting. Particularly praiseworthy is the fact that it, along with several motion picture versions of Ramona's story, has certainly served to bring the Cahuilla Indians to the attention of thousands of people who otherwise would never have known that these interesting people existed.

The publication in 1884 of Helen Hunt Jackson's *Ramona* had such a profound effect upon the Indians of California, and especially upon the Cahuilla, that something about the author and her writing of the novel may not be out of place.

As detailed in Chapter II, Mrs. Jackson had long been interested in the sad plight of the American Indian, and this had led to her writing *A Century of Dishonor*. This factual account of the abuses which had been inflicted upon the red man had awakened some interest in the Indian question among a few influential people, but it had not in any way stirred the public conscience. However, it did lead to her being appointed in 1882, with Mr. Abbott Kinney, to make a survey of conditions among the Mission Indians of California. She included the report of that survey, made to the Commissioner of Indian affairs,

in every edition of *A Century of Dishonor* published after
1883

While in southern California on this survey Mrs. Jackson was a frequent guest at Carmelita, the Pasadena home of Mrs. Ezra Slocum Carr, the same Mrs. Carr who for so many years gave encouragement to the efforts of John Muir. Those who knew the two women well felt that it was a discussion in Mrs. Carr's home that fired Mrs. Jackson with the idea of attempting a novel about southern California in which she would stress the tragic situation of the Indians there. Once she acquired this idea she seems to have become obsessed with it.

In the course of her work Mrs. Jackson came to San Jacinto and there met a Miss Mary Sheriff who was teaching among the Soboba Indians. Miss Sheriff told her a tragic story about two young Cahuilla, Ramona Lubo and her husband Juan Diego. The woman with whom Mrs. Jackson boarded, Mrs. J. C. Jordan, gave her further details of the cruel affair. It was this story of the brutal and unwarranted killing of Juan Diego by a white man, Sam Temple, called Farrar in the book, that proved the long-looked-for point of fact around which could be crystallized the experiences and previously unrelated facts that she had picked up in her studies. *Ramona* was born.

Upon her return to the East she worked steadily on her theme, constantly writing letters to California friends asking for items of information which would enrich and verify the story she had in mind. Knowing the wealth of factual material she drew upon and used one can forgive the public for tending to accept fiction as fact and fact as fiction.

The success of *Ramona* was immediate. It was hailed as the "great American novel" and quickly became a best-seller. Since 1884 it has appeared in edition after edition. With her novel Mrs. Jackson truly succeeded in arousing public indignation over the inhuman treatment to which the red man was subjected in the 1800's. Moreover, as a result of the success of *Ramona* her report on the Mission Indians was accorded far greater attention than it would have received otherwise. In fairly short order reservations were set aside for the remnants of the tribes that had managed to suvive more than "a century of dishonor."

It would be wrong to give the impression that with the publication of *Ramona* California Indians entered into a period of political and economic security. Unhappily the frontier psychology still existed in most of the Southwest, and ruthless exploitation of the Indian continued to be carried on in many places with total disregard for law, ethics, or plain common decency.

Readers will recall that *Ramona* opens with a sheep-shearing scene. This episode probably stemmed from visits Mrs. Jackson had made to Camulos Rancho, for many years the property of the del Valle family. Located a few miles west of Saugus, this ranch was maintained by the del Valles in the manner and style of the best of the old California ranches. Indeed the Moreno Rancho of *Ramona* is an almost photographic description of Camulos.

It was our privilege to visit Camulos many times while the del Valles were still in residence there. It was from Mr. U. F. del Valle that we first heard of the Cahuilla Indians. He told us of bands of Cahuilla that occasionally journeyed all the way to Camulos to help with the sheep-shearing—California's first migratory workers! He spoke in praise of their independence, their intelligence, and their integrity.

The Ramona of Mrs. Jackson's novel is half Gabrieleño Indian and half Scotch. Doubtless, as Ramona's father, the novelist had in mind that well-known Scot of an earlier California period, Hugo Reid. In nearly every case the characters of the novel are patterned after actual people. The Mrs. Jordan of San Jacinto, for instance, became the Aunt Ri of *Ramona*.

Of the true Ramona we know almost nothing, up to the time of the death of her husband Juan Diego, except that she was a woman of the Mountain Cahuilla group. Photographs taken of her in later years show her to be a typical Cahuilla, heavy featured and heavy set, but a person of dignity and intelligence.

The fictional husband of Ramona, Alessandro, was depicted by Mrs. Jackson as a Luiseño Indian whose father was the *Capitan*, or chief, of the Indians of San Luis Rey Mission. In reality, Juan Diego, the Indian husband of Ramona Lubo, was a Mountain Cahuilla who often went down from the mountains to work at odd jobs around the town of San Jacinto. This Juan Diego was known to early settlers chiefly for the occasional mental lapses that caused him to do erratic things. Once he was discovered happily riding a properly saddled cottonwood log. Once, while herding goats for Will Tripp, he, apparently unknowing what he did, drove them far out on the desert. However, in general he was regarded as honest and as a good workman.

Juan Diego and Ramona Lubo and their small child had a cabin, a garden, and a few fruit trees, by a spring in the flats that lie between Mt. Cahuilla and Little Cahuilla Mountain back of the Indian settlement of that day—near the present town of Anza. This little valley is still known as Juan Diego Flats.

By way of noting the parallels of fact and fiction which Mrs. Jackson made use of it may be interesting to compare two accounts of the incident which fired her to write *Ramona*. This is the way she described the actual killing of Juan Diego in the report she made in 1883 to the then Commissioner of Affairs:

A Cahuilla Indian named Juan Diego had built for himself a house and cultivated a small patch of ground on a high mountain ledge a few miles north of the village. Here he lived alone with his wife and baby. He had been for some years what the Indians called a "locoed" Indian, being at times crazy; never dangerous, but yet certainly insane for longer or shorter periods. His condition was known to the agent, who told us that he had feared he would be obliged to shut Juan up if he did not get better. It was also well known throughout the neighboring country, as we found on repeated inquiry. Everybody knew that Juan Diego was "locoed." (This expression comes from the effect a weed of that name has upon horses, making them wild and unmanageable.) Juan Diego had been off to work at sheep-shearing. He came home at night riding a strange horse. His wife exclaimed, "Why, whose horse is that?" Juan looked at the horse, and replied confusedly, "Where is my horse, then?" The woman, much frightened, said, "You must take that horse right back; they will say you stole it." Juan replied that he would as soon as he had rested, threw himself down and fell asleep. From this sleep he was awakened by the barking of the dogs, and ran out of the house to see what it meant. The woman followed, and was the only witness to what then occurred. A white man, named Temple, the owner of the horse which Juan had ridden home, rode up, and on seeing Juan poured out a volley of oaths, levelled his gun and shot him dead. After Juan had fallen on the ground Temple rode closer and fired three more shots in the body, one in the forehead, one in the cheek, and one in the wrist,

106

the woman looking on. He then took his horse which was standing tied in front of the house, and rode away. The woman, with her baby on her back, ran to the Cahuilla village and told what had happened. This was in the night. At dawn the Indians went over to the place, brought the murdered man's body to the village and buried it.

This is how Mrs. Jackson makes use of the finale of this tragic episode in her novel *Ramona*:

When she went into the house, Alessandro was asleep. Ramona glanced at the sun. It was already in the western sky. By no possibility could Alessandro go to Farrar's and back before dark. She was on the point of waking him, when a furious barking from Captain and the dogs roused him instantly from his sleep, and springing to his feet, he ran out to see what it meant. In a moment more Ramona followed—only a moment, hardly a moment; but when she reached the threshold, it was to hear a gunshot, to see Alessandro fall to the ground, to see, in the same second, a ruffianly man leap from his horse, and standing over Alessandro's body, fire his pistol again, once, twice, into the forehead, cheek. Then with a volley of oaths, each word of which seemed to Ramona's reeling senses to fill the air with a sound like thunder, he untied the black horse from the post where Ramona had fastened him, and leaping into his saddle again, galloped away, leading the horse. As he rode away, he shook his fist at Ramona, who was kneeling on the ground, striving to lift Alessandro's head, and to stanch the blood flowing from the ghastly wounds. "That'll teach you damned Indians to leave off stealing our horses!" he cried, and with another volley of terrible oaths was out of sight. . . .

. . . waves of grief broke over her, and she sobbed convulsively; but still she shed no tears. Suddenly she sprang to her feet and looked wildly around. The sun was not many hours high. Whither should she go for help? The old Indian woman had gone away with the sheep, and would not be back until dark. Alessandro must not lie there on the ground. To whom should she go? To walk to Saboba was out of the question. There was another Indian village nearer—the village of the Cahuillas, on one of the high plateaus of San Jacinto. She had once been there. Could she find that trail now? She must try. There was no human help nearer.

It is obvious from these two excerpts that it is almost impossible to say where fact ends and fiction begins.

Small wonder then that readers and audiences at the pageant accept fiction for fact, and vice versa!

The astonishing popularity of *Ramona* catapulted the living original of the novel into the full glare of public attention. More and more travelers to California sought out Ramona Lubo—to buy her baskets, to talk with her about the novel, to point up to the mountains where she and her husband and child had lived, for she had not chosen to return to the scene of the tragedy. She lived out her life in the home of her brother, Cinciona Lubo, near the Indian settlement known as Cahuilla, doing laundry work for the women of Judge S. V. Tripp's family, whose extensive ranch was adjacent to Juan Diego Flats.

Years after Juan Diego's death Ramona Lubo gave birth to another child, a boy she named Condino. From all accounts he was a bright, pleasant youngster to whom Ramona was devoted. When harassed by questions from white visitors as to who was the father of this child, with typical Indian humor she would answer with the name of any man, white or red, that happened to pop into her head. This provoked some amusing complications as more and more whites came into the area who were not at all familiar with the facts of the case or with Indian psychology and humor.

As Condino himself grew older he helped himself to the name Hopkins, the name of a white man whom he knew and admired—which proved an added complication on occasion. Eventually Condino moved down into the town of San Jacinto where on March 7, 1907, it is recorded that he married an Indian girl with the incongruous name of Marta Kline. In its account of his wedding the newspaper of that day reports that both the bride and the groom had had a grammar school education, that Condino had been well instructed in farming and in stock raising, that he had tourmaline mines in the mountains, and a thousand shares in a copper mine at Bisbee, Arizona!

George Wharton James, that prolific writer who by old-timers was sometimes referred to as "George Whopper James," became a virtually self-appointed press agent for Ramona Lubo. James did have a very genuine interest in and sympathy for the Indians of the Southwest and lectured about them tirelessly and wrote about them copiously. Ramona was a "natural" for his attentions, and words about her flowed from his pen. He even brought to her home one of the primitive cylinder phonographs of his day and persuaded her to speak into the horn and make a record of her version of the killing of Juan Diego.

Ramona Lubo died on July 21, 1922, while visiting in San Jacinto Valley. She was buried beside Juan Diego in the old Cahuilla cemetery in the San Jacinto Mountains. A wide mountain meadow is all that separates their graves from the foot of the range in which she and Juan Diego had built their home and where he had been killed thirty-nine years before. In 1938 the Ramona Pageant Association placed permanent markers on the graves, cut granite blocks surmounted with white stone crosses.

Behind the cemetery looms a picturesque mass of eroded granite rocks in which a few crude petroglyphs have been cut. Here and there one can find a bedrock mortar once used for the grinding of acorns and other seeds. Below the cemetery a large pool of water is constantly fed by an ever flowing hot spring. Here one can frequently find small Cahuilla youngsters, the Ramonas and Juan Diegos of today, bathing and playing in the warm water as have the Cahuilla of all time.

There are no descendants of Ramona and Juan Diego at Juan Diego Flats today. The small open valley high up between Cahuilla and Little Cahuilla Mountains is now in white man's hands. Electricity and propane gas bring the comforts of easy living even here. A legend has grown up, however, that the land is cursed and that nothing will grow where Juan Diego's blood was spilled.

Nowadays pageants and playgrounds, streets and schools, cities and convents, freeways and farms, all bear the name Ramona. Who can say whether the name honors the tragic heroine of Helen Hunt Jackson's novel or the equally tragic Ramona Lubo?

Certain it is, if it had not been for the strange quirk of fate that prompted a young San Jacinto school teacher to voice her indignation over the needless, brutal killing of a harmless Cahuilla Indian, the real Ramona would have lived out her life in obscurity and the history of the Cahuilla Indians would undoubtedly have been a different, and perhaps a more tragic, story.

DURING THE TURBULENT mixed-up days of the 1840's, '50's, and early '60's California was twisted and torn by revolt, war, conquest, and factional disputes. Too often law and order went by the board, and crimes of violence were punished with sadistic cruelty by those leaders, white and Indian, who were responsible for what semblance of authority existed. Even today there is scarcely a page of the history of that period which is not the subject of heated controversy among historians, be they amateur or professional.

In the records of those decades no California Indian is so well assured of a place as is "Captain-General" Juan Antonio of the Mountain Cahuilla. Almost nothing is known of his early years, but by the mid-century he had emerged as a powerful leader of his branch of the Cahuilla. His stout figure was, and is, as controversial as the period in which he flourished, but to his people he was, and still is, a hero.

It has been repeatedly said that Juan Antonio was leader of all the Indians from San Timoteo Canyon and the San Jacinto Mountains to the land of the Yumas by the Colorado River. This, however, is a point difficult to verify. In discussing the matter with Guadalupe Lugo of the present-day Mountain Cahuilla we mentioned that there seemed to be no way of proving it.

"Lupy" then offered as proof the story that Juan Antonio had had three branding irons made so that all the Indians under his jurisdiction could brand their cattle with his brand. One of these irons was given to the Cahuilla of the desert, one to the Cahuilla at Old Santa Rosa, and the third to the Cahuilla living in the valleys and mountains around what is now the town of Anza.

"That may be," we said, "but where are those branding irons today?"

Without a word old Guadalupe got to his feet and started toward his barn, gesturing to me to follow him. There hanging among a number of branding irons, new and old, was an ancient-looking one bearing a conjoined JA.

"Given to us by Juan Antonio himself," said "Lupy" proudly.

There was no doubt in his mind that "Captain-General" was a title fully merited by Juan Antonio.

To those who feared and/or hated Indians Juan Antonio seemed a cruel despot. Stories, in the main unverified, are told of how he buried a murderer alive with the corpse of his victim, and of how he cropped off the ears of two Indian boys found guilty of stealing. Whether true or false these stories must be viewed in proper perspective. If the gentle Franciscans of the Missions could countenance ear-cropping, facial branding, and the use of the lash on their Indians, can we, in all honesty, be critical of a "heathen" Indian who may have been following the example of the "civilized" white man?

We first come to know Juan Antonio as guardian of the holdings of the Spanish-California Lugo family, at that time one of the largest land-owners in southern California, with extensive acreage in San Bernardino Valley. By the early 1840's raids upon the Spanish-California ranchos by hostile Indians from the Colorado River area, and from as far away as Utah, had become an unbearable menace. To protect their holdings against these raiders the Lugos enlisted the services of Juan Antonio and a group of Indians from the San Jacinto Mountains.

These Mountain Cahuilla established themselves at a place known as *Politana* on the Santa Ana River wash, near the present town of Colton. Armed only with their potent bows and arrows, for some years they did valiant service in guarding not only the Lugo properties but also those of other rancheros in the area.

Juan Antonio's loyalty to such famous Californios as the Lugos did not keep him from participating in a Fourth of July celebration eight years before California was a state of the United States. Daniel Sexton, a onetime mountain man, was cutting timber in San Gorgonio Pass in 1842. He got nostalgic when the "4th" rolled around in a region where, naturally, there was no celebration of Independence Day. He decided to do something about it on his own, so he invited Juan Antonio and his Cahuilla to join him in a barbecue in Edgar Canyon, the main feature of which seems to have been the broaching of two barrels of whiskey! The fiesta was climaxed by the raising of the first American flag to fly against the California sky.

When war broke out between the United States and Mexico the Lugos and Juan Antonio found themselves embroiled in it in a way typical of the confusion of the time. Eleven of General Andreas Pico's men were captured by some Luiseño and other Indians hostile to the Spanish-Californians, and they were taken to the settlement at Warner's Ranch, where the Indians held a council to decide what to do with them. A renegade sailor living at the ranch, one William Marshall, persuaded the Indians that the Americans would no doubt be happy indeed if the Spanish-Californians were put to death, which the Indians proceeded to do in horrible fashion. Whereupon General José Maria Flores, the Californian commander, delegated José del Carmen Lugo to pursue and punish the assassins.

Lugo left Los Angeles with fifteen men, and at Politana they were joined by Juan Antonio and fifty of his Cahuilla fighting men. This avenging party ambushed the Luiseño and their allies at Aguanga, killing a number of them and capturing the others. The captives were placed in the custody of Juan Antonio, who promptly killed every one of them.

Lugo censured the Cahuilla chief for this needless cruelty. Juan Antonio explained that Lugo was a captain of white men and he, Juan Antonio was a captain of Indians—and that made a difference. If those other Indians had captured him and his Cahuilla, he declared, they would have roasted every one of them alive!

During the winter of 1850-51 the famous Ute chief, Walkara, and a large band of warriors made extensive raids on the herds of the great ranches of the south. Entering California by way of Cajon Pass they penetrated as far as Claremont and Azusa. When Walkara drove off a large band of particularly fine horses belonging to José Maria Lugo, Juan Antonio once more went into action. He and his men, together with Lugo and other rancheros, pursued the warlike Utes through Cajon Pass all the way to the Mohave River.

In April 1851 there arrived in southern California a former captain of the cavalry of the United States, John Irving, and with him a band of heavily armed desperadoes, including a number of Australian convicts who in some mysterious fashion had made their way to the gold fields. This rabble stayed in and around Los Angeles for about two months, raising all kinds of hell.

Two young members of the Lugo family, grandsons of Antonio Maria Lugo, had been jailed on a murder charge, later disproved. Irving went to the old man and offered, for five thousand dollars, to break open the Los Angeles jail, free the young men, and take them to Mexico. Old Lugo sternly refused to consent to this, saying that his lawyer would handle the matter in proper legal fashion. Irving was infuriated and vowed revenge on the Lugos.

Shortly afterward this lawless gang made plans to go to Mexico to seize one of the silver trains which in those days travelled between Chihuahua and Mazatlan. When they learned that by this time the young Lugos had been legally freed and were at their ranch near San Bernardino they plotted to stop at the ranch on the way, help themselves to the best of the Lugo horses, kidnap the young men and hold them for a ransom of ten thousand dollars.

Somehow word of Irving's plans got out, and the sheriff of Los Angeles sought the help of General J. H. Bean, then in charge of the United States forces in southern California. The sheriff and a large posse rode to Camp Dolores, not far from Politana, where Bean had a party of volunteer rangers, and warned Bean of Irving's plans. They determined to try to intercept Irving at Rincon, but Irving took a different route from the one originally set and got to the Lugo ranch.

When José del Carmen Lugo saw the marauding gang arriving he despatched a vaquero for Juan Antonio. By the time Juan Antonio and his fighting Cahuilla rode into the ranch the Irving lot were pillaging the ranch house. Upon seeing Juan Antonio and his warrior force the pillagers left in a hurry, heading for San Jacinto by way of Yucaipa. Juan Antonio lost no time in overtaking them, for he and his Indians knew the lay of the land.

Irving had trained his men well, and they charged the Cahuilla in efficient cavalry fashion, firing their revolvers as the Indians came at them. The Indians, although still armed only with bows and arrows, were more than a match for them. They engaged in a sort of running warfare of harassment and retreat and finally succeeded in driving the outlaws into Live Oak Canyon, where it crosses San Timoteo Canyon, and up an old wood-road which ended in heavy chaparral. There the Irving gang was trapped.

At this point Indians from other nearby settlements joined Juan Antonio for the kill, and kill they did—only one outlaw managed to survive, by hiding in the thick underbrush.

General Bean, who by this time had caught up with Juan Antonio, was now furious that white men—even such lawless ones as Irving and his motley crew—should have been killed by Indians! He made such serious threats against Juan Antonio and his Cahuilla as to cause them to leave Politana and move back to their villages in the San Jacinto Mountains.

General Bean's attitude that not even an outlaw—if he were white—should be killed by an Indian demonstrates the bitter feeling against the red man that was such a part of frontier psychology.

Later the coroner came from Los Angeles, accompanied by County Attorney Benjamin Hayes, and held an inquest into the deaths of Irving and his gang. Their verdict was that the killing of the whites by the Cahuilla was completely justified. The authorities are said to have awarded one hundred dollars' worth of supplies to Juan Antonio for the elimination of Irving and his outlaw horde.

Before the year was over Juan Antonio and his people were persuaded by the Lugos to return to Politana, and again Juan Antonio was to prove his loyalty to the white man and carve for himself another important niche in the colorful history of California.

During the previous year some ill-advised officials of San Diego decided that an easy way to collect more taxes would be to levy on the Indians of the back country. The Indians, of course, were not consulted, and resentment was widespread. In 1850, most unwillingly, they paid up to the tune of about six hundred dollars. Then General Bean arrived on the scene and advised the Cupeño Indians at Warner's Ranch not to pay. Sheriff Agoston Haraszthy was forced to attempt to collect from the recalcitrant red men, but both the Cupeño and the Luiseño chiefs sent word that they would not pay. Then, reluctantly, the sheriff notified the Indians that if they failed to pay he would be forced to come with enough men to drive off and sell their stock in lieu of the tax.

Among the Indians who held their ground was Antonio Garra, a Cupeño Indian. Garra had been educated at San Luis Rey Mission and seems to have been appointed as some sort of go-between between his people and American officialdom. He and his son, also named Antonio Garra, were living at the Indian village at Warner's when the tax trouble started. Also living there, with the daughter of José Nocar, an Indian leader, was the renegade sailor, William Marshall, referred to earlier.

Garra and his son determined to engineer a general uprising against the whites by all the Indians in southern California, and all summer and fall they were busy seeking the support of various leaders, including Juan Antonio. Marshall is said to have urged Garra to try to get the backing of the Spanish-Californians against the newcomer Americans, but this facet of the revolt failed to secure support.

Unlike the better-planned Pueblo Indian Revolt against the Spaniards in New Mexico, word of the projected Garra revolt leaked out. Rumors were a dime a dozen from Santa Barbara to San Diego. The general belief was that the Indians planned to kill every white—man, woman, and child—from San Bernardino to the sea, down the length of the southern part of the state. Word was current that even the masterful Cahuilla of the deserts and mountains were armed and ready for revolt.

There was good reason for the whites to be alarmed, for at that time they were in the minority in most of southern California. Should Juan Antonio and his Cahuilla join in the revolt the carnage would, without doubt, be fearful. The Mormon settlers in San Bernardino Valley retired behind a fort-like stockade. Every ranch prepared for the attack. The question in everyone's mind was—would Juan Antonio join Antonio Garra or would he remain loyal to the white man?

General Bean was now placed on the spot. Being in charge of the United States forces in California he had to take the field against Garra and the Indians for doing the very thing he had earlier advised them to do, *i.e.*, refuse to pay taxes. On December 4 he led his forces from Los Angeles in the direction of Cahuilla territory. That same day Duff G. Weaver, who had a ranch in San Gorgonio Pass near that of his brother Paulino, received a taunting note from Garra which determined him to seek the help of Juan Antonio, with whom he was on good terms.

At this critical point Juan Antonio took his stand with the Americans, and a sigh of relief went up from all the whites roundabout. Weaver supplied the Cahuilla leader and his warriors with horses and supplies and urged Juan Antonio to go after Garra.

The Cahuilla rode virtually into Garra's camp. Juan Antonio then sent a note to Garra urging him to come to the Cahuilla camp. When Garra did so, he was made prisoner. Within a short time young Garra with ten Indians, their women and children, surrendered at the Duff Weaver ranch, where they were unmercifully taunted by the Cahuilla. Young Garra became so enraged by their mockery that he knifed Juan Antonio through the arm and side. This precipitated an attack upon the prisoners by the Cahuilla, which might have proved a massacre had not General Bean arrived in time to prevent it.

With the capture of both Garras the back of the Indian revolt was broken. Among those tried for treason were William Marshall and old Garra. Both were found guilty. Marshall was hanged in San Diego. A note in a San Diego paper of the time has this to say of Garra's end: "No man could have met his fate in a more grave and dignified manner than did Antonio Garra. He had been led to an open grave in Old Town, blindfolded and made to kneel. A squad of riflemen riddled the kneeling man with well-aimed balls."

This time the work of Juan Antonio brought commendation from General Bean. The officer gave the Indian leader and his men valuable presents and also—absolutely without authority to do so—drew up a treaty "of peace and amity and friendship between the people of the State of California to protect and maintain Juan Antonio in the possession and occupation of his lands, property and effects so long as he continues to act in a friendly manner toward the American people."

In 1852 at Temecula Juan Antonio and other Indian leaders signed with Dr. O. M. Wozencraft, then Commissioner of Indian Affairs, a treaty under which the United States was to set aside for the exclusive use of the Indians concerned a tract of land about forty miles wide and thirty miles long between San Gorgonio Pass and Warner's Ranch. This treaty seems to have been signed in good faith by all concerned, but it was never properly ratified. The Indians, not understanding that ratification was necessary, later were confused and bitter when the provisions of the treaty were not fulfilled.

Juan Antonio then moved with his people to the spot in San Timoteo Canyon known as Sahatapa, and continued on excellent terms of understanding with the neighboring whites and with the Mormon colonists who were swarming into San Bernardino Valley. Even in 1853, however, the Mormons were still living within the stockade they had built during the threatening days of the Garra revolt! In return for the friendly, helpful attitude which they have usually taken toward Indians the Mormons gained the cooperation of Juan Antonio in defense of their farms against marauders.

But not many years were to pass before the treaty Juan Antonio had signed with Commissioner Wozencraft began to be violated by both hostile Indians and lawless whites. In November 1855 some Mormons made complaint to their church officials in San Bernardino that the Cahuilla were committing depredations and had made some unfriendly demonstrations. By this time Captain Juan Antonio had been breveted "General" by General Stephen W. Kearny, and been designated "Captain-General" by the superintendent of Indian affairs. So it was to him, in San Timoteo Canyon, that there came a delegation of Mormon settlers, backed by a strong force of United States army men. They found him deeply resentful of a dozen American families that had settled on Cahuilla lands without their permission. He asked what had become of the plows, hoes, spades, and other agricultural tools that had been promised them.

Captain H. S. Burton of the United States Army made a report on the Cahuilla situation. In it he stated that the Cahuilla then numbered thirty-five hundred males, of whom fifeen hundred were fighting men. He expressed his alarm at the position of power that "Captain-General" Juan Antonio had among them. Nor was he the only one that was alarmed. It is said that even some of the more tractable Indians of the San Gorgonio Pass area spoke of Juan Antonio as *Yampooche*—he who gets mad quickly. There was added consternation when it was discovered that Juan Antonio was in some sort of communication with the Mohave-Apache and the Yuma. Was another revolt in the making?

The Mormon settlers joined with army officers in a show of force and followed this with a genuine attempt to adjust the grievances of the Cahuilla, for Juan Antonio and his group at Sahatapa were indeed in an unfortunate situation. White settlers were taking up land here, there, and everywhere. Mormon missionaries were zealously trying to make converts among the Indians, whom they believed to be Lamanites, descendants of one of the lost tribes of Israel. Non-Mormon settlers were bitter in their feeling against the Mormons. The more confused the situation grew, the more the Cahuilla looked to Juan Antonio for leadership and the more the better element among the whites accepted him as spokesman for the Indians.

It had become an accepted procedure that when an Indian committed any sort of crime against the whites he was to be turned over to Juan Antonio for trial and punishment. In turn Juan Antonio had agreed that any white man he caught doing wrong would be turned over to the white authorities. He established a regular court in which he acted as judge. When an offender was to be tried a jury was impanelled, the accused was given right of counsel, and witnesses were summoned by both sides. Court procedure was followed with great solemnity—indeed it is said that the dignity of this Cahuilla Indian court more than matched that of many a white man's court of the era.

Once a Cahuilla Indian, who had killed a fellow tribesman, had been arrested by the sheriff and put in jail in San Bernardino. When Juan Antonio got news of this he promptly gathered together about forty of his men and, mounted on horses, mules, and burros, they rode to the residence of County Judge A. D. Boren. There they de-

manded that the Cahuilla prisoner be turned over to
them for trial.

Judge Boren did not have legal authority to do this so
he referred Juan Antonio to Justice Valentine J. Herring
—"Uncle Rube" Herring—who asked Juan Antonio to
make a statement. The speech he made on this occasion
bears out his reputation as an orator. It was made in a
solemn, impressive manner in his own language and was
translated for the *San Bernardino Weekly Patriot* of December 7, 1861, as follows:

Judges, Captains, and Gentlemen of San Bernardino.—I come not
here as a child to play, but as an old gray-haired chief to transact business and talk with white man. I come because my people asked me;
they sent for me. I was far away from my village when they came and
told me that murders were being charged upon my people. I took some
of my old men who do not steal and murder, and came a long way to
meet you. On our way we caught an Indian who murdered a Sonoranian
named Antonio. But we being few in number, last night he made his
escape. But my Indians are on his trail, and he cannot escape if he
remains in the Indian country. He is a bad Indian and should be hung.
I am an American—my people are all Americans, although we are Indians. If we should hear of armed men in these mountains, we should
come and tell you, and help fight with you. This is our country, and it
is yours. We are your friends; we want you to be ours.

Some of my people are bad men and commit crimes. But all are not
bad. He alone should be punished who murders and steals; he should
pay all the debt. If the Governor of the United States should say my
people are all bad, and must be killed, then you should kill us. But the
Governor does not say so, and he never will. He sends warriors to
fight for all of us. That is the reason they are here now. My people
come here to the white people, and walk about, and white men give
them whiskey, and then they try to get their squaws, and then they
fight. My people are buried all around, killed by white men. I shall take
my people away from this place, and then there will be no more of this.
When white men want Indians to work, they can come and get a recom-
mend from our village, and then they will get good men. Now I want
when one of my people commits a crime, to have him punished. I will

124

deliver up any white man who commits crime to be dealt with by his people, and I wish to punish my people my own way. If they deserve hanging I will hang them. If a white man deserves hanging, let the white men hang him. I am done.

"Uncle Rube" Herring was enough impressed by the old man's dignity and sincerity to order that the Cahuilla prisoner be released and turned over to him. Incidentally, this seems to be the only available record of any of the many eloquent pleas made by the "Captain-General."

The reporter of this graphic occasion describes Juan Antonio as "stout of body, scarcely five feet four inches tall—short and thick—wiry even in old age, and with an aspect about the eyes, nose, and brow that came nearer to that of the African lion than I have ever seen in another human face."

In those troubled days Juan Antonio often must have gazed up at his San Jacinto Mountains and wondered whether he and his people might not be better off at *Coos-woot-na,* his clan home high in the mountains. If such an urge to return there ever came to the old man it is regrettable indeed that he did not act upon it, for soon tragedy was to strike his people and himself.

In the autumn of 1862 an epidemic of smallpox hit Los Angeles and it spread with the utmost rapidity throughout all of southern California. Undertaking establishments were hard put to take care of the bodies of the dead. Apparently no attempt was made to vaccinate the Indians, and the death toll among them was fearful—their rancherias in many instances were depopulated, and the general population was decimated.

Panic swept Juan Antonio's village in San Timoteo Canyon and many of the Cahuilla left there for their mountain homes or to join Cahuilla clans in San Gorgonio Pass or on the desert. Thus the infection spread, and its effects were so devastating that the Cahuilla never really recovered to reassume the powerful place they once had held.

Juan Antonio himself fell victim to the disease and tried to treat himself in the only way he knew, with sweat baths in his lodge, followed by plunges into ice-cold water. Duff Weaver, hearing that the old man was ill and deserted by his panic-stricken people, did what he could for him, hiring a Mexican, who for some reason was known to be immune to the disease, to take him food and to give him what comfort he could. The old lion of the Cahuilla seemed to sense that his life was nearing its end, and he dragged himself out of his hut to die alone under the open sky.

The *Los Angeles Star* of February 28, 1863, carried a report by Benjamin Hayes, by that time District Judge, which adds a sorry commentary upon the passing of the old chief. It contains these bitter words: "Old Juan Antonio and four other Indians have died of smallpox and I have been informed that the bodies have not been buried and that they are being mutilated by hogs and dogs. Of course it is a matter of much annoyance to the whites in that neighborhood. Where is our Indian agent?"

In this ignoble fashion death came to the noble chief of the Cahuilla. Within a few years the Cahuilla lands in San Timoteo Canyon had been taken over by white settlers.

Is there a California Indian to match Juan Antonio in loyalty, in intelligence, in courage, in leadership? What monument can attest the worth of such a man?

The Judge Benjamin Hayes, mentioned above, seems to have pondered this question, too. One day he looked up at the massif of the San Jacintos from a point near the rancho called Jucumba, west of present-day Redlands. Then in his diary he recorded these words:

"... We know little of this gigantic heap, a *terra incognita*. An Indian rancheria, said to be well-governed, is somewhere there. Familiar as I am with Indians, I have never seen a soul that belongs to it. Realm of mystery! What spirits of the ancient heathen tribes are guarding it from invasion? Is there no legend to tell? I only remember that its sands are of gold on the further side . . . There [Juan Antonio] was born eighty years ago, I have heard. Let it be his monument—Chief, whose stern deeds are all the history thy people have, or all till now told of them."

IX

FIG TREE JOHN OF THE DESERT Cahuilla was a "character," something of an achievement in a state replete with "characters." San Franciscans boast a rich variety of stories about their "Emperor Norton," but I feel sure that old-timers of the Colorado Desert could more than match those stories with tales—tall and otherwise—about Fig Tree John.

Almost every pioneer of Coachella Valley has his favorite anecdote about Fig Tree, and as the years go by they have mounted into quite a legend, nothing having been lost in the re-telling. The shade of Fig Tree John must get many a chuckle from these endlessly repeated narratives about him, for, like most Cahuilla, he had a poker-faced sense of humor.

As with Ramona and Juan Antonio there is considerable difference of opinion concerning Fig Tree John. Some of it stems from a novel about him by the late Edwin Corle. That this was a work of fiction seems to have been lost sight of by many. The old Indian, whose name is the title of the book, was obviously the prototype of Corle's fictional hero, but an inconclusive incident led Corle to the idea that Fig Tree John was an Apache who had taken sanctuary in California.

The story goes that one day a white man friend of Fig Tree brought an acquaintance with him on a visit to the Indian. This casual visitor thought that Fig Tree looked like an Apache and he spoke a few words of Apache which Fig Tree *seemed* to understand. This was the slim evidence upon which the story of his Apache origin was based.

There is incontestable proof that Fig Tree John was a Cahuilla Indian. He was a member of the clan commonly known as the Agua Dulce clan. Strong, in his *Aboriginal Society in Southern California*, gives the name of this clan as *Wantcinakak Tamianawitcem*.

Fig Tree John himself preferred to be known by the Spanish name of Juanita Razon, and he insisted that it was Juanit*a* and not Juanit*o*. Early survey parties into Coachella Valley found Fig Tree and his family living in an arrowweed jacal-type house at a spring near Salton

130

Sea. In some way he had gotten hold of cuttings of the black California Mission fig and had planted them around the spring, where they grew well. These fig trees and his Spanish first name, Juanita, readily led to his being dubbed "Fig Tree John."

Fig Tree John's son, known to the whites of the region as Johnny Mack and sometimes as Young Fig Tree John, claimed that his father had been born near the spring which came to bear his name. Although the Southern Pacific Railroad had been granted ownership of the section of land where Fig Tree lived, it never questioned his right to live there. In fact, when the Colorado River broke through in 1905 and re-flooded the Salton Sea, the railroad made not the slightest protest when Fig Tree began to reap a financial harvest by salvaging ties from the flooded railroad and selling them to the ranchers around Mecca, who badly needed good fence posts.

As more and more people came into Coachella Valley Fig Tree began to fear that he might lose his land. Armed with an ancient Winchester—which had lost some of the parts essential to its ever actually being fired—the old man assumed a most belligerent attitude and ordered any trespassers off his property. This led to his being rated a pretty tough character.

Those who knew him best never felt this way about him. Miss Cornelia B. White of Palm Springs once made a long desert trip with him and found him to be a most trustworthy individual, as well as an excellent guide. There are stories, too, of his kindness on many occasions to both whites and Indians who staggered into his oasis, suffering from thirst and other discomforts which even today can be incident to desert travel.

Most of the white settlers around Mecca were fond of the old man. When he could no longer make hunting trips into the Santa Rosa Mountains or secure adequate food from desert plants or from his own garden, they were more than generous in trading with him. For the melons, figs, etc., which he grew with considerable success they made liberal exchange for such basic foods as flour, sugar, and coffee.

Fig Tree always had a string of horses, and he was a shrewd trader. Having made the sale of a horse to some passing prospector, Fig Tree and his wife then rode into the general store at Mecca. There he made his purchases carefully, item by item, and paid for them with the proceeds of the sale, often in native gold dust or small nuggets. This gave rise to the belief that he had a secret gold mine in the Santa Rosas. Even today an occasional adventurer sets out to find the "lost" gold mine of Fig Tree John.

Around 1910 Fig Tree acquired a buggy which from then on he and his wife used on their trips into town and to the various Indian ceremonies or "fiestas." At some earlier period he had acquired the impressive costume which he always wore on such occasions. This consisted of an ancient coat with large military buttons with "Connecticut" on them, and a battered old top hat.

Where he got hold of these astonishing garments is one of the Fig Tree John mysteries. Some say that he had once acted as guide for Fremont and was presented with the outfit at the conclusion of his employment. His son, Johnny Mack, claimed that the fantastic clothes had been given to his father at an Indian meeting of some sort in Los Angeles.

Ridiculous as this costume sounds, old Fig Tree wore it with the utmost dignity and aplomb. Naturally he was in constant demand for photographs and sketches, and from this source he was able to add considerably to his income.

Fig Tree John died on the reservation at Martinez on April 11, 1927, and was buried in the Catholic cemetery there. There has been much speculation as to how old he was at his death. His son maintained that he was 136. Mrs. Nina Paul Shumway in her excellent account of Fig Tree John in *Desert Magazine* of January 1941 said that to her his feet, rather than his face, were indicative of great age, that they "were horny and splayed like an eagle's."

How long Fig Tree John lived is not so important as that he so lived as to be a legend in his own time and long thereafter.

TODAY SYLVESTER COSTO, direct descendant of the great "Captain General" Juan Antonio of Cahuilla yesterdays, drives the big yellow school bus which conveys the boys and girls, both Indian and white, from the Cahuilla valley region around Anza all the way down to Hemet High School and back. He is a trustworthy and highly respected member of that mountain community and is Master of the local Grange.

Harry Hopkins, grandson of Ramona Lubo, lives in a charming house in Cherry Valley back of Beaumont. The house was a war surplus structure which Mr. Hopkins bought and moved to his own lot. He protests that he is no carpenter, but with rare ingenuity and good taste he rebuilt and repainted and landscaped the original shabby house so that it is now one of the most attractive homes in the region. Mr. Hopkins also has a most attractive home in the desert, and recently he was elected chairman of the Torres-Martinez Tribal Council.

These two descendants of the two most famous Cahuilla Indians typify the adaptability of people of Cahuilla blood and exemplify their successful adjustment to the many changes wrought by the vast tidal wave of white settlers that flooded their land. It speaks well for the intelligence and the stability of the Cahuilla that relatively few of them were swept into the discard by that tidal wave and by the series of injustices to which they were subjected by some white settlers and by many ignorant and corrupt officials. To vault within the space of about a hundred years from a primitive culture of taboos and witchcraft to the complex American culture of today is certainly no mean feat.

In some cases, it is true, Cahuilla have been unable to take the step from their old way of life with its sparse household economy of baskets, pottery jars, metates and manos, to today's gadget economy. This in part explains the reservation house which all too often is surrounded by a sad litter of dead automobiles, broken and discarded pots and pans, and ill-used household furnishings.

The emergence from the stark simplicity of the old days into the mechanized complexities of today has been too sudden to enable some Cahuilla to develop an adequate sense of relative values. This inadequacy is evident in the occasional squalid reservation shack with an up-to-date television antenna mounted on the roof and a sleek chrome-encrusted automobile parked amidst the litter of the front yard.

* * * *

During the half century that followed Helen Hunt Jackson's *A Century of Dishonor* conditions for the Cahuilla—and for American Indians in general—were little better. Too often Indian lands were ruthlessly taken over and "homesteaded" by white settlers. Schemes of every shade of dubiousness were undertaken to keep the red man "in his place." Even after reservations were established boundary lines were still conveniently "floated" so as to exclude from Indian control a valuable spring, a fertile meadow, or a possible mineral deposit.

A century and a half of dishonor ended in a new deal for the Indian under the administration of Herbert Hoover. Many of the reforms inaugurated during those years came to fruition in the Indian Reorganization Act passed by Congress in 1934 at the beginning of the Roosevelt administration. Although many of the provisions of this act have not been accepted by certain groups of Indians, it was a great step forward, granting for the Indian improved educational facilities and opportunities for him to attain a position of respect and human dignity.

The Indian Reorganization Act made it possible for tribal groups to set up and direct their own local governments and to form corporations for various business purposes. The Act also set up a revolving credit fund to enable them to get on their feet economically. As a result some groups have been able to buy back and return to tribal ownership lands which previously had been allotted to individuals.

The Act is under almost constant attack—by white men who resent the Indians being able to take into their own hands many fields of activity which in the past had been remunerative to the white man, and by the Indians themselves. The Indian's objections to certain facets of the act stem from his lack of understanding of the purposes of the Act. Often, too, the Indian Bureau has failed to properly prepare and train those Indians who did take advantage of the act to launch into business endeavors, endeavors for which they had no previous experience or training and even lacked personal adequacy. In such circumstances failure was inevitable. Considering the broad picture, it is reassuring and, in some cases, downright inspiring to see the success that many Indians have attained under the Act.

The Indian Reorganization Act has made it possible for various Cahuilla Indian groups to set up Tribal Councils for the government and management of their affairs. Some of these Tribal Councils have wrestled, and are still wrestling, with problems pertaining to lands and water rights, in many cases problems more complex than any other American Indian group has had to face.

The Sacramento Office of the Bureau of Indian Affairs has jurisdiction over all the reservations in California. According to the records of this office there are Indians of Cahuilla blood only on the following reservations: Agua Caliente, Augustine, Cabazon, Cahuilla, Santa Rosa, Soboba, and Torres-Martinez. However, we have learned from various informants that Indians with at least some measure of Cahuilla blood are also to be found on the Morongo and Los Coyotes Reservations.

It must be kept in mind that many, if not most, of the Indians on the reservations mentioned do not think of themselves as Cahuilla, because they do not agree with, or do not know of, the anthropological classification of peoples according to language roots. Indian Bureau officials often have had scant training in anthropology, or any interest in it. As a result confusion has been compounded, and misunderstandings and disagreements constantly arise between the Indians and federal, state, and local officials. Indeed so tangled and so confused and confusing is the Cahuilla situation today that one is forced to admire the patience and skill of the few dedicated officials and Tribal Council members who have worked to bring some just order out of the chaotic mess.

One of the complicating factors is the intelligent stubbornness of the Cahuilla. They have been tricked and defrauded so many times in the past that they are now trebly suspicious of every proposition that is presented to their Tribal Councils for consideration. Then, too, like their Shoshonean cousins, the Hopi of Arizona, the Cahuilla are rugged individualists. This leads them into many schismatic groups and makes "tribal" policy difficult to establish and maintain. Sometimes one cannot help but feel that an assembly of a dozen Cahuilla means a dozen different viewpoints on the matter up for discussion.

This inability to agree and to work together for the common good is a sad handicap to them in the development of such economic potentials as their lands may have.

* * * *

The majority of the Cahuilla still live on their reservations. In some cases they may not live there the year around, nevertheless they still hold rights to the land there.

At first glance life today on a Cahuilla Indian Reservavation is not much different from what it is anywhere else. Since 1924 the Indian has been a citizen of the United States. In still more recent years the restrictions against his purchasing liquor have been removed. County and state services in California have gradually been extended to apply to all Indians. When an Indian breaks the law he is arrested by the local police officer and put into the same jail as is his badly-behaved white brother. Indian children go to the public schools. As reservation lands pay no taxes, the school district is reimbursed, under Public Law 874, just as it is for those youngsters attending school from such other nontaxed lands as national parks, armed services reservations, and the like.

When the Indian Bureau inaugurated its land allotment plan, reservation lands were to be divided up into individual allotments which were to be turned over to "competent" Indians. At once it ran into a series of com-

140

plications. On what basis was an Indian to be judged competent or incompetent? Just what is an Indian anyway?

It is rather amusing to find that even today the Indian Bureau has not yet come up with an acceptable definition of what makes an Indian. According to testimony given on one occasion by Mr. Leonard M. Hill, Area Director of the Sacramento office of the Bureau of Indian Affairs, for some purposes any person living on reservation lands and having at least one quarter Indian blood is an Indian. However, when the various Tribal Councils began to make up their tribal rolls in preparation for the present plan for termination of Indian Bureau guardianship they found it necessary, on humanitarian grounds, to consider as Indians many persons who certainly had a great deal less than one quarter Indian blood.

To judge competence was an even harder nut to crack. Until quite recently educational opportunities for some Cahuilla were both spotty and variable. Many a smart youngster never had an opportunity to get an education compatible with his ability. Should he as an adult be considered incompetent? If age is to be the criterion of competence how can a line be drawn? Few white men want to feel that they are incompetent at 65! How is the age of an Indian to be determined anyway, when Indian vital statistics have been kept in such haphazard fashion, if at all?

The greatest handicaps to reservation life in Cahuilla country are the aridity of the land, the lack of opportunity for gainful employment, isolation, lack of sanitation, and the difficulty of obtaining financing for improvements.

At this point it may be of value to give a brief survey of the reservations in southern California where Indians of Cahuilla extraction live or where they have vested interests. The figures of reservation acreage, allotments, and population are taken from the progress report for 1955 made by the (California) Senate Interim Committee on California Indian Affairs.

All of these reservations are in Riverside County except Los Coyotes Reservation, which is in San Diego County. Los Coyotes Reservation has a population of 25 and over 25,050 acres, none of which is allotted. In San Diego County mention should also be made of Santa Ysabel Reservation. Some of the 40 people who live there may have some degree of Cahuilla blood. None of the 9,679 acres of this reservation is allotted.

In alphabetical order the first of the Riverside County reservations is the *Agua Caliente Reservation*. This reservation comprises 31,128 acres of which 2,961 acres have been allotted to individuals. These lands are located in the city of Palm Springs and also include the highly scenic canyons back of the city. There are about 80 Indians in the Agua Caliente group. The reservation gets its name from the famous hot springs which still flow in the very heart of the sophisticated modern city of Palm Springs.

Incidentally, this Agua Caliente band should not be confused with the one often referred to in history books on southern California. The latter lived near the springs which we now know as Warner Hot Springs.

Augustine Reservation is near the town of Thermal in Coachella Valley, and is named after "Captain" Augustine, an old Indian leader of the region. 154 of its 616 acres have been allotted. Its population is 8.

Cabazon Reservation, near Indio, is named for old "Chief" Cabazon, whose village was at the entrance to Painted Canyon. This reservation has a population of 15 and contains 1489 acres of which 320 acres have been allotted. Much of this land would be well suited to agriculture if water were available.

Cahuilla Reservation, near Anza, has a population of 32. None of its 18,272 acres has been allotted.

Morongo Reservation, east of Banning, covers 31,724 acres of which 1427 acres have been allotted. There is a population of 125, but, because of extensive intermarriage with the Serrano, the Chemehuevi, and possibly other Indians who share this reservation, it is virtually impossible to tell how many of the 125 can be considered Cahuilla. Within the last few years the Morongo Tribal Council has contracted for the sale of peat from a bog in a mountain valley within the reservation.

Ramona Reservation is a very small reservation of 520 acres high on the slope of Thomas Mountain in the San Jacinto Range. No Indians live on this reservation, but Cahuilla from the Anza region and from Valle Vista run a few cattle here in the summer.

Santa Rosa Reservation is in the mountains back of Palm Desert. It comprises 11,733 acres of which none has been individually allotted. A few Indians live here at times during the summer, but their permanent residence is in Valle Vista or elsewhere nearby. The area is used largely for the running of cattle.

Torres-Martinez Reservation has a population of about 250 and is thus the most populous of the reservations concerned with those of Cahuilla blood. It is situated near Thermal. There are 30,132 acres in this reservation and of these 8,550 acres have been allotted. About 9000 acres have been inundated by the rise of the Salton Sea in recent years. About 10,000 of the reservation's acres would be excellent agricultural land if Colorado River water, to which the Indians have rights, could now be made available to them for irrigation. Good water is also undoubtedly available from the underground flow from Martinez Canyon.

In several areas in southern California the Cahuilla have become so completely integrated with the general population that neither they nor their neighbors are in any way conscious of their being a "minority group."

* * * *

Reservation acreage which has been allotted to individuals can be sold by its owners, but only through procedures under Indian Bureau supervision. Of lands which have not been allotted to individuals the Tribal Council of the reservation can assign certain acres for individual use, but title to this acreage remains with the government. Upon the death of the assignee the acreage reverts either to the Tribal Council for reassignment or to the Indian Bureau. Because they have no title to such assigned lands the Indians have, naturally, been reluctant to make extensive improvements on them even when they are financially able to do so.

We may sympathize with and applaud the determination of a few present-day Cahuilla to try to preserve what fragments of the old customs and songs and ceremonies they still cherish. The fact remains, however, that the breaking up of tribally-owned reservation lands into individual allotments and the sale or granting of long-time leases of such lands will inevitably, in the long run, bring about the absolute extinction of even these remnants of their life of yesterday.

One cannot blame the Bureau of Indian Affairs for this. The real tribal community and ceremonial life had very largely disappeared from the various Cahuilla bands long before the Bureau decided upon policies looking toward termination of federal control of Indian affairs.

❊ ❊ ❊ ❊

Of all the Cahuilla the handful of people comprising the Agua Caliente band of Palm Springs are, of course, the most fortunate from an economic standpoint. When their reservation was established in 1876 the area was looked upon by the whites of that day as just so much worthless desert. No one then could possibly have foreseen the plush resort community of today where some Indian holdings in the downtown area are worth thousands a front foot. To watch the alert, well-groomed Agua Caliente Tribal Council is, to realize that here are Indians who will not be trading Palm Canyon for a string of shell beads.

It is curious that today women play such important roles on the various tribal councils and business committees. There have been occasions when entire tribal councils were made up of women. This must seem enigmatic indeed to those whites who, erroneously, have always believed that woman's place in an Indian community was that of an overworked slave, a beast of burden in comparison with her indolent lord-and-master husband.

In contrast with the wealth that has come to the Agua Caliente people are the sere, barren, rocky wastes of the Morongo, Los Coyotes, Cahuilla, and Santa Rosa Reservations. These speak only too eloquently of the poverty of most of the Indians who are attempting to eke out a living in these areas. Some of the Indian shacks in the country around the little town of Anza are a distressing sight. There may be a few trees surrounding the house, making a small oasis in the otherwise drear landscape, but in the valley below a giant sprinkler may be throwing life-giving circles of water over the acres of a white rancher, although no blame must be attached to him. He certainly is not responsible for whatever actions, ethical or otherwise, took his choice lands from the Indians who originally possessed them.

In 1883 Helen Hunt Jackson visited the leading Mountain Cahuilla village of this region, a village called Cahuilla in those days. She wrote that at that time it had a population of from one hundred fifty to two hundred Indians. They had sixteen fields, large and small, under cultivation and were living in adobe houses with thatched roofs. They raised wheat, barley, corn, squashes, and watermelons—although there was but one plow in the village! Many of them owned cattle. Mrs. Jackson described the women as "neatly dressed, the children especially so, and the faces of all, men, women, and children, had an animation and look of intellectual keenness very uncommon among the Southern California Indians.

146

On the outskirts of the village is a never-failing hot spring. In this water the Indians, old and young, are said to be continually bathing."

The hot spring is still there, and it is still in almost constant use for bathing—but where are the fields? Where is the village?

One can only hope that the day will come when the lands still in Indian possession, either as individual allotments or in tribal ownership, can be developed to their full economic potential. It gives some scant reassurance that at long long last electricity has been made available to some parts of the local reservations.

It seems most unfortunate that, when the rights of the Coachella Valley Cahuilla Indians to Colorado River water were established recently, no financial plan was worked out to enable them to take advantage of these rights. Now the liens for this water are piling up, for the Indians do not have the capital to develop their lands by using the water. They may well be forced to sell out and thus lose all rights to their tribal heritage.

We have been given to understand that there is considerable land still in the hands of the Mountain Cahuilla for which water is available. Might not some sort of Mountain Cahuilla cooperative be organized which would make it possible for them to make proper use of the water in developing their land?

Despite the many handicaps, so corrosive to the human spirit, under which the Indians of Cahuilla blood have existed, it is reassurng to see that so many of them have surmounted the obstacles put in their paths. To talk with them even briefly is to become conscious of their intelligence, their individual integrity, and their fine sense of humor. They have their full share of the poor in spirit—the drunks and the improvident—but they are regarded by the Cahuilla as a disgrace to their people, as similar drunks and improvidents are regarded by their own people eveywhere—be they black, brown, red, or white. The astonishing thing is that there are relatively few of them among the Cahuilla.

✶ ✶ ✶ ✶

Much needs to be done on all the reservations we have considered. The long-drawn-out controversies regarding water development on every reservation, except possibly the Agua Caliente, certainly should be brought to an equitable conclusion. Ways and means of bettering the economic status of those Indians who desire to remain on their own lands could and should be worked out. A program of better housing and sanitation is long overdue.

It is to be hoped that the Agua Caliente Tribal Council will work out some cooperative agreement with the National Park Service for the preservation of the priceless areas of Palm and Andreas Canyons which are still controlled by this group. These are two of the most beautiful desert canyons in our country. Access roads and picnic areas are at present maintained by this Tribal Council, and a small admission fee is charged to all visitors. A few years ago a devastating fire swept through Palm Canyon. This was a tragedy that must not be repeated if there is any adequate means of prevention.

White neighbors of Indians in the Palm Springs area have done much to help by their honest, straightforward, friendly interest. A similar neighborhood policy on the part of white neighbors of the Cahuilla everywhere would be a most constructive move.

The American Friends Service Committe has done yeoman service in working to develop a better understanding between Indians and whites. It always stands ready to offer guidance and assistance when called upon to do so, without any attempt to win converts. The Friends do good for the sake of doing good. They rarely hand out food and second-hand clothing to the Indian. Instead they work to help the Indian achieve an independent status that will enable him to purchase his own food and clothing.

❋ ❋ ❋ ❋

The program to end federal supervision over Indian affairs is a highly controversial matter. During the century that the administration of Indian affairs by the Indian Bureau was a constant public scandal it was natural that friends of the Indian should come to feel that the abolishment of the Bureau could not help but be a blessing for the Indian. However, many, if not all, the national organizations interested in Indian welfare are opposed to unqualified ending of federal supervision.

They point out that the government has not fulfilled its treaties and its ethical obligations to work out a program to help the Indians help themselves. Today many Indians are leaving the reservations of their own free will, thus "emancipating" themselves without any help from Uncle Sam. Today, too, there is no great problem so far as assimilation is concerned. The problem that remains is that of the reservation Indian. He should be taught, not necessarily the white man's way of doing things, but how to develop the possibilities of his lands. This is a responsibility that the government has no right to slough off.

Many of the intelligent white friends of the Indian feel that the breaking up of reservation lands into individual allotments should be opposed, on the basis that these reservation lands have always been held in common —much as the white man's corporation holds lands in some instances. It is felt that if the Indian desires to continue to hold land in this way he certainly should be privileged to do so.

The administration of Indian affairs is a highly complex matter, and there is no single over-all solution that can possibly be satisfactory to all. A plan that may be excellent for the Apache may be totally inacceptable to the Zuni. The intricate patchwork of indigenous languages, traditions, and customs among the American Indians is certainly indicative of how impossible it is to generalize about policies with regard to them.

The problem becomes even more complex when the Cahuilla are considered. Here we have a people who were never a tribe in the generally accepted meaning of that word. Instead they have always lived in more or less isolated, independent village bands. So what might be a satisfactory administrative plan for the Agua Caliente band might not work at all for the clans of the Cahuilla living around present-day Anza. Because they are highly individualistic people, a plan that suits Jack Lo may not be at all suitable for Pete Lo. And what about the Cahuilla that do not live on Cahuilla lands at all but have

150

moved to Indio, Beaumont, Riverside, or Los Angeles? It
is small wonder that the direction and management of
Cahuilla affairs have brought aches to red and white
heads alike!

❋　❋　❋　❋

California history is more colorful and picturesque
because of the many pages upon which the Cahuilla have
written their names. The courage, integrity, intelligence,
imagination, tenacity, pungent sense of humor, and dra-
matic flair, which distinguished such Cahuilla of the past
as Fig Tree John, Cabazon, Juan Antonio, and Ramona,
are evident in their descendants who are among us today.
It is not unreasonable to expect that from a people who
in the past possessed folk lore of such poetic quality, and
whose stone tools, baskets, pottery, and mats were of such
a high order of craftsmanship, there will emerge creative
artists who will make significant contributions to the cultural life of the Southwest of today and of many tomor-
rows.

Certainly Indians who were able to triumph over so
inimical an environment as that of the Cahuilla, and who,
in less than one hundred years, could rise from a primitive society of seed-gatherers and hunters with bow and
arrow to take their place in today's complex world, have
earned the right to be considered California's "master"
tribe.

151

FIG TREE JOHN
—Photo, Field Studios, Riverside, Calif.

DOMINGO COSTO
Great Grandson of Juan Antonio

154

MRS. KATHERINE SIVA SAUBEL
President of Malki Museum and tribal council
member of Los Coyotes Reservation

—Photo by Weazy Wold

155

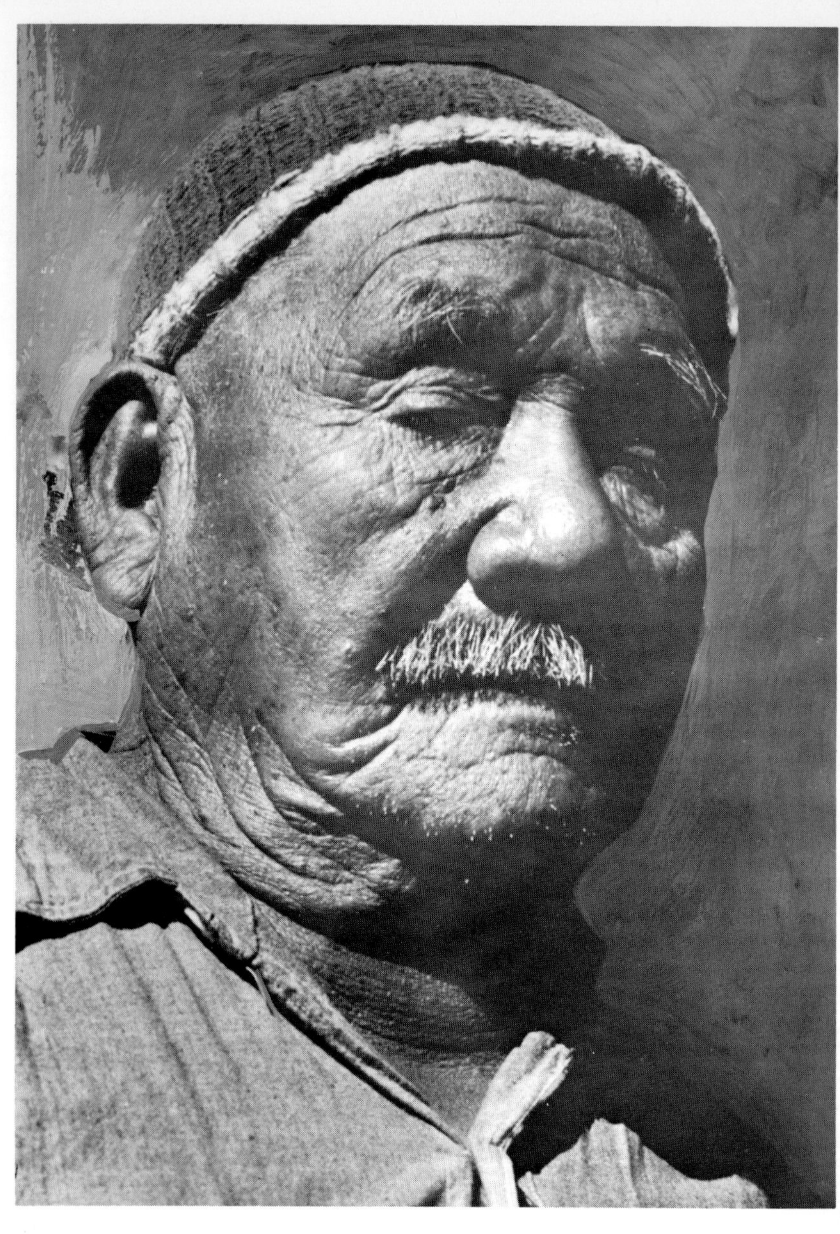

"CAPTAIN" LOUIS LEVI
Father of "Captain" William Levi
Both ceremonial leaders of the Desert Cahuilla

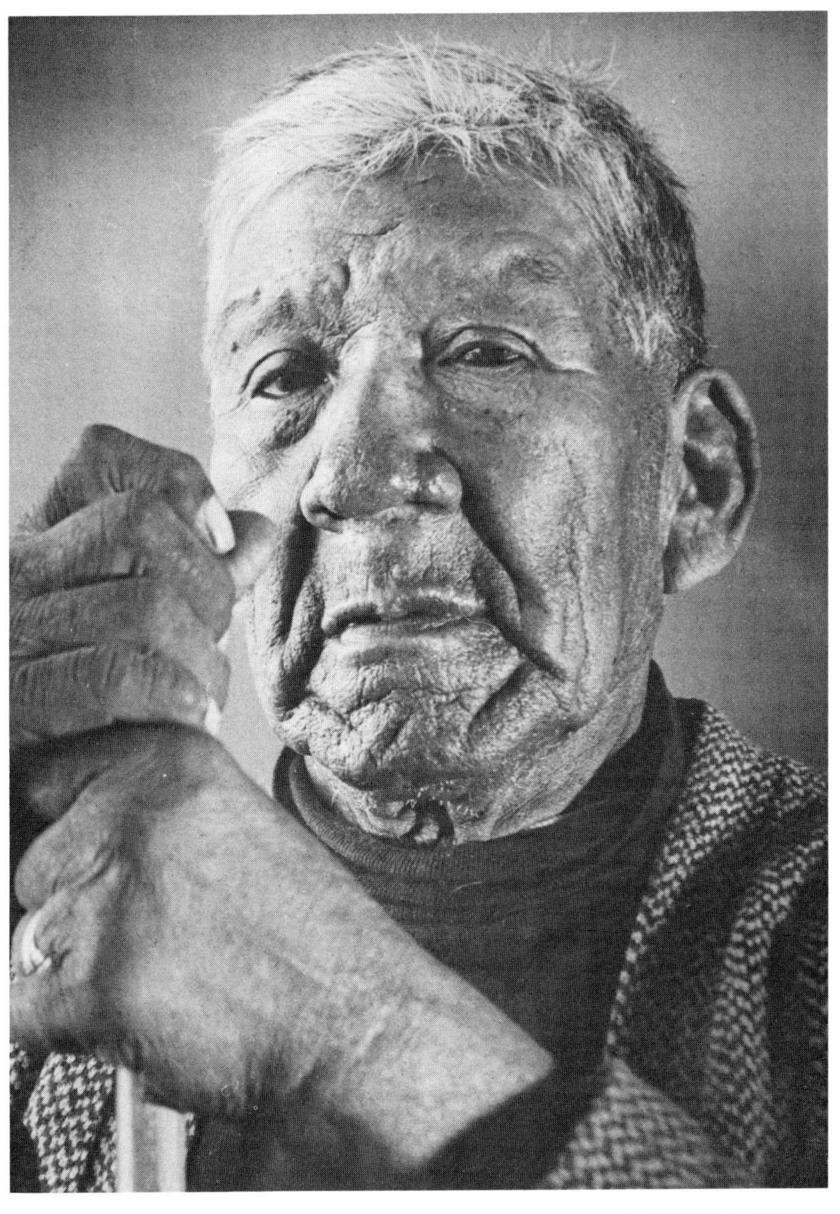

CALISTRO LUGO
Well-known Indian citizen of Palm Springs, a nephew
of the famous Desert Cahuilla Indian "Fig Tree John."
—*Val Samuelson Photo*

AMBROSIA
One of the last of the Desert Cahuilla "fire-eaters"
—Photo by Avery Edwin Field

158

MRS. LEE ARENAS
Cahuilla Basket-maker
—From photographic archives of the
Southwest Museum, Los Angeles, Calif.

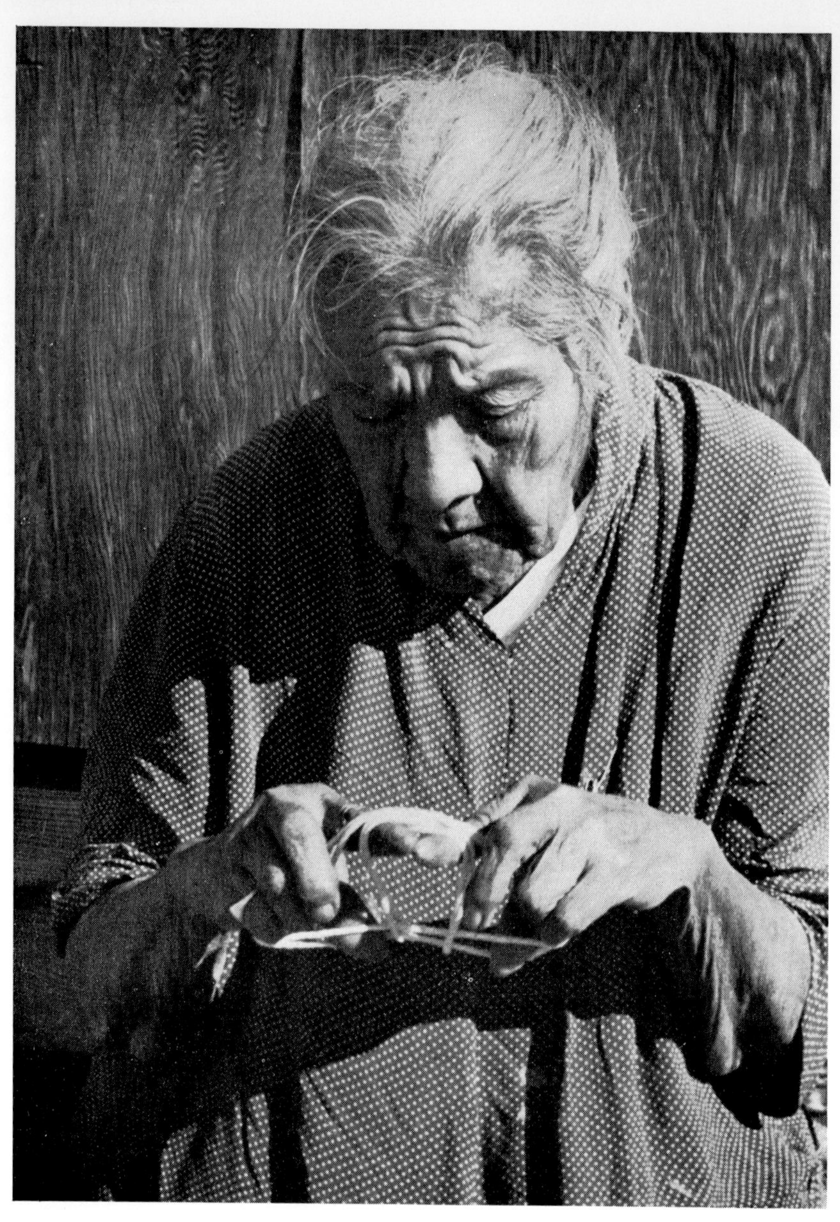

MRS. VICTORIA WEIRICK
demonstrates the forms of Cahuilla
cat's cradle used to prophesy the
sex of an unborn child

160

CALISTRO TORTES
Sauishpakiktum leader of the
Santa Rosa Reservation

CEREMONIAL HOUSE
of the late "Captain" William Levi of Torres-Martinez

On the death of Captain Levi, during the summer
of 1958, this building and his home were both burned
to the ground according to Cahuilla custom

PABLO COSTO
Grandson of Juan Antonio, who was said to
resemble the old Captain very closely
*—Photo courtesy Dr. Gerald Smith
and San Bernardino County Museum*

164

THE REAL RAMONA
—Photo courtesy of the San Bernardino County Museum

JANE PABLO PENN
Wanakik Cahuilla, daughter of Cahuilla leader
William Pablo, and founding trustee and
director of Malki Museum

Photo by Weazy Wold
166

FRANCISCO NOMBRE
Francisco, of the Desert Cahuilla, lived for more than
thirty years at Puichekiva (Roadrunner's House)

CAHUILLA CEMETERY *(upper)*
GRAVES OF RAMONA AND JUAN DIEGO *(lower)*
—*Photos by Val Samuelson*

168

(*upper*) MT. CAHUILLA (NEAR ANZA)
Juan Diego Flat lies beyond the summit
(*lower*) GUADALUPE LUGO AND HIS GRANDSON
Pointing out to the author the place in the San Jacinto
Mountains where Ramona and Juan Diego lived
—*Photos, Val Samuelson*

169

SYLVESTER COSTO
direct descendant of Juan Antonio, drives the
big school bus from Anza to Hemet
every school day in the year

HARRY HOPKINS
grandson of Ramona

SALVADOR LOPEZ
One of the last Desert Cahuilla "fire-eaters"

IGNACIO SEGUNDO
Blind medicine man of the Mountain Cahuilla
who, during his later years, lived at Palm Springs
—*Southwest Museum Photo*

CAHUILLA DESERT HOUSE WITH
BASKET GRANARIES ON THE ROOF

AN INDIAN WELL OF
THE DESERT CAHUILLA

BASKET GRANARIES

Carl Eytel knew the desert Cahuilla and they knew and liked him. Eytel came to the Cahuilla country as a young man in the 1890's. His sensitivity, his modesty and his abiding love for the desert soon won him lasting friendships among both the early white settlers and the Indians. As an artist he was largely self-taught and his finest work was undoubtedly in his small pen and ink sketches.

Early in the 1900's George Wharton James secured a multitude of these to illustrate his *Wonders of The Colorado Desert* and it is because of Eytel's sketches that the book is now something of a collector's item. James pays Eytel generous praise in the book but desert gossip has it that Eytel received far from generous remuneration for his work.

These few of his Cahuilla sketches are from the originals now in the collection of The Southwest Museum.

OLLAS

SUNSET TIME
Rosa and Marcos Belardo of the Agua Caliente band
—*Photo by J. Smeaton Chase and used with Mrs. Chase's permission.
Courtesy, Palm Springs Desert Museum and Historical Society.*

176

APPENDIX

Dr. John P. Harrington, of the Bureau of American Ethnology in Washington D. C., is considered one of the preeminent authorities on the Indians of California. Some years ago Dr. Harrington annotated the now almost priceless Fine Arts Press edition of Father Boscana's account of the Southern California Indians. That worthy Franciscan very naturally felt that he must lift a chiding finger and add a few words to show his disapproval of the heathen Indian way of life. He was very shocked by their scant attire and writes of it as "clothing if it can so be called."

This prudish statement by Boscana seems to have gotten quite a rise out of Dr. Harrington for he annotates that line as follows:

"The old Indians all testified that going free from clothes, living the outdoor life, plenty of exercise, little close work and Indian grub made for extreme longevity and a life with lots of fun all the time. Colds were exceedingly rare, tuberculosis, piles, cancer, and venereal diseases absent, so the oldest informants have stated, informants who really knew. The household rose at daylight and all its members headed, the year round, for a plunge in the nearest water, preferably at an hour so early that Wuyoot, the Moon, resurrected Indian god, would still be looking at them. 'So the Moon would get to see you clean,' old Francisco Calac of Pala used to say.

"For raising children there was nothing like it. It reduced the work and the worry to one-fourth, and the expense to merely that of the food. There was no scolding: 'Now, Johnny, don't get your feet wet, and don't get down in the dirt.' The kids could wallow in the mud all day, could play throwing it at each other, could climb trees without a rip, wrestle without losing a button, and could play sliding down great sleek rocks, as they often did, without fear of wearing out anything but their own behinds. Instead of playing dressing up they painted up. There was no making or buying of clothes for the youngsters, no washing, no mending and as for spanking one did not even have the trouble of letting their pants down. Whatever bit them or got the matter with them, the trouble was in instant and constant sight. Furthermore, the custom was most democratic for the children of the poor or lazy looked as handsome as those of the rich. Even as the poor benighted Hindoo (of the old rhyme) these people made their skins do.

"With all our dentistry, the Indians suffered not one tenth the pain with their teeth that we do. With all our agriculture and stock raising, the Indians ate more wholesome food than we do. With all our blaze of electric lights and all our motion-pictures, the Indians lived lives more preservative of their eyesight than we do. With all our radios, the Indians rested their ears to the sounds of nature and got equal pleasure. With all our books and bibles, the Indians got supreme delight from the handing down of aural knowledge. With all our architects, the Indians lived in healthier houses and communities that were earthquake proof. With all our superior knowledge about drugs, the Indians who gave us tobacco, did not smoke tobacco to one twentieth the extent that we do. With all our books, the barbarous toloache-using Indians were a thousand times more temperate. With all our automotive vehicles and beasts of burden, the Indians had as good a time in merely walking around the country, and with results far less damaging to their anatomy. With all our clothing industry, at which men slave away their lives, the Indians, without clothes, suffered less from heat and cold and from the results of heating and chilling the body than we do.

"In writing about the Indians it is sometimes refreshing for a moment to forget our rigid standpoint of superiority and to dream our way back into simple customs, which under-population made possible, and to praise them."

BIBLIOGRAPHY

MATERIAL about the Cahuilla Indians is to be found, with few if any exceptions, only in the larger libraries and, occasionally, in bookstores dealing with western Americana. In the paragraphs which follow the writer comments briefly on sources which he has found of value in the preparation of his book.

THE ETHNO-BOTANY OF THE COAHUILLA INDIANS OF SOUTHERN CALIFORNIA, by David Prescott Barrows. University of Chicago Press. 1900.
Without question this Barrows monograph is one of the most informative of the writings about the Cahuilla. It was written as a dissertation for the degree of doctor of philosophy. Later Barrows became a potent factor in the life of California as president of the University of California. As long as he lived he remembered, with nostalgic affection, the days he spent among the Cahuilla Indians.

ABORIGINAL SOCIETY IN SOUTHERN CALIFORNIA, by William Duncan Strong. University of California Press. Berkeley. 1929.
This magnificent work deals not only with the Cahuilla, but also with their neighboring tribes—the Serrano, the Cupeño, and the Luiseño. It is without doubt the most complete account of these Indians

available today. Unfortunately it is out of print and can be found only by diligent search.

The Cahuilla Indians, by Lucile Hooper. University of California Press. Berkeley. 1920.

Next to Strong's book mentioned above this is the most modern book about the Cahuilla. Although it is not as broad in scope as *Aboriginal Society*, it is an ideal supplement to it.

Life in California, by Alfred Robinson. Biobooks. Oakland. 1947.

This book was first published in 1846 by Wiley and Putnam of New York. It is important here because the second part of the book is Robinson's translation of the account of the Chinigchinich cult by Friar Geronimo Boscana of San Juan Capistrano Mission. Boscana's account, found among his effects after his death in 1831, is *the* source material on this cult which had such far-reaching influences upon the Indians of southern California.

The Fine Arts Press of Santa Ana brought out the Chinigchinich portion of Robinson's book in rather spectacular format. This edition also contains the valuable, and often very witty, notes of Dr. John P. Harrington, the eminent ethnologist.

Handbook of the Indians of California, by A. L. Kroeber. Bulletin 78 of the Bureau of American Ethnology of the Smithsonian Institution. 1925. Re-issued in a photolithographic facsimile edition by the California Book Company. Berkeley. 1953.

Kroeber's work is the classic one on the Indians of California and is pre-eminent as source material. The later studies of Hooper and Strong, made, we presume, under Dr. Kroeber's guidance, have corrected some, if not all, of the inevitable errors in the earlier work.

Pioneer Notes from the Diaries of Judge Benjamin Hayes. Privately printed. Los Angeles. 1929.

In these notes, which cover the years 1849-1875, Judge Hayes makes considerable mention of Juan Antonio. Hayes was a highly intelligent man and an excellent observer, in addition to being possibly the best-educated man of his day in southern California. He had a rare sense of appreciation of the Indians of his part of the state, the Cahuilla among them.

The Heritage of the Valley, by George William Beattie and Helen Pruitt Beattie. Biobooks. Oakland. 1951.

This is without doubt one of the finest of local histories. Much of the material in it about the Cahuilla and Juan Antonio was obtained from the diaries of Judge Benjamin Hayes.

SHOSHONEAN DAYS, by G. Hazen Shinn. Privately printed for the author. The Arthur H. Clark Company. Glendale. 1941.

Shinn came to Colton when quite a young man and later made frequent visits to Captain John Morongo and his wife Rosa at the Indian settlement near Banning. The book is a record of his experiences from 1885 to 1889.

INDIANS OF SOUTHERN CALIFORNIA, by Dr. Ruth Underhill. Sherman pamphlets No. 2. Haskell Press. Lawrence, Kansas.

In this fifty-cent pamphlet Dr. Underhill has written an excellent popular account of the Indian tribes of southern California, with some attention given to the Cahuilla. It is beautifully illustrated with photographs and with drawings by Herrera.

STORIES AND LEGENDS OF THE PALM SPRINGS INDIANS, by Chief Francisco Patencio as told to Margaret Boynton. Privately printed. Los Angeles. 1943.

This book should be read only after one has familiarized himself with the work of Strong, Hooper, Kroeber, etc. By the time Patencio told his stories and his experiences to Margaret Boynton so much extraneous material had crept into his accounts as to make it difficult indeed to sieve the wheat from the chaff. However, the little book does contain some interesting legends about certain places in the eastern end of Coachella Valley and in the San Jacinto Mountains.

CALIFORNIA DESERT TRAILS, by J. Smeaton Chase. Houghton Mifflin Company. 1919.

This truly classic account of the Colorado Desert has references to things Cahuilla scattered throughout its three hundred eighty-seven pages.

THE INDIANS OF SOUTHERN CALIFORNIA OF 1852, edited by John Caughey. Huntington Library. San Marino. 1952.

This book is sub-titled "The B. D. Wilson Report and a Selection of contemporary comment." The "B. D. Wilson Report" is that of "Don Benito" on the Indians of southern California, made when he was appointed "sub-agent" for the tribes of this area. He was assisted in the writing of the report by—indeed some say the whole report was written by—Judge Benjamin Hayes.

183

A Century of Dishonor, by Helen Hunt Jackson was first published by Roberts Brothers in 1885. In the editions published after 1905 the appendix was devoted to Mrs. Jackson's report on the Indians of California with frequent mention of the Cahuilla.

A Bibliography of the Cahuilla Indians of California, by Lowell John Bean and Harry W. Lawton. Malki Museum Press, Banning, 1967.

This Land Was Theirs, by Wendell Oswalt. John Wiley and Sons, Inc., New York, 1967.

Cahuilla Ethnobotanical Notes, by Lowell Bean and Katherine Siva Saubel. Surv. Ann. Rept., Univ. Calif., Los Angeles, 1960-61: 237-245; 1962-63: 51-78.

Diaries and Accounts of the Romero Expeditions in Arizona and California, 1822-26. Palm Springs Desert Museum, 1962.

The books of George Wharton James, particularly *The Wonders of the Colorado Desert* and *Through Ramona's Country* have in them much of interest pertaining to the Cahuilla, but, unfortunately, James' fancy often ran away with him and played strange tricks with the facts.

His Colorado Desert book is valuable for its many sketches of Cahuilla life made by Carl Eytel, a young German artist. Carl Eytel is the only white man, so far as the writer knows, who was permitted burial, by the Agua Caliente band, in the Cahuilla cemetery in Palm Springs. The Cahuilla had great affection for him.

THE DECORATIONS
by DON LOUIS PERCEVAL

DRAWINGS MADE FROM CAHUILLA PICTOGRAPHS
IN THE SAN JACINTO MOUNTAINS

Drawings made from Cahuilla baskets in the collections in S.W.M., The Southwest Museum, Los Angeles, California; P.S.D.M., The Palm Springs Desert Museum, Palm Springs, California; or N.P.S., the collection of Mrs. Nina Paul Shumway, Palm Springs, California

THE AUTHOR ...

Harry C. James was born in Ottawa, Canada, but has been a citizen of the United States for many years. After completing his studies at the Collegiate Institute in Ottawa, he did special work at Queen's College in Hamilton. In World War I he served with the Canadian Engineers.

At the close of hostilities he came to Hollywood, California, where he established a small club for boys interested in his great interest—the outdoors. His club expanded into The Trailfinders organization and the Trailfinders School for Boys. For twenty-five years he served as its headmaster, until the school was sold in 1950. As founder-president of The Trailfinders he continues the camping and conservation activities of the organization from its present headquarters at the Lolomi Lodge, in the San Jacinto Mountains—once the mountain stronghold of the Cahuillas.

From the beginning he has taken a deep and abiding interest in the Indians of the Southwest—particularly the Hopis, and the tragic remnants of the once numerous Cahuillas. Widely known and beloved by them, he makes frequent visits to their villages and homes. He writes and lectures about them as a person who is truly one of them.

In addition to many magazine and newspaper articles about the Hopi and Cahuilla, he has written the following books: "Red Man-White Man," "The Hopi Indians," "The Treasure of the Hopitu," "Haliksai!," and now this fine book about his nearest neighbors "The Cahuilla Indians."

THE ILLUSTRATOR ...

Don Louis Perceval, illustrator of "The Cahuilla Indians," was born in England but grew up in Southern California. He attended Hollywood High School and studied at the Chouinard Institute of Art. In the summer of 1928 he attended the Heatherley School of Art in London, and then on to the Royal College of Art, 1928-31. He camped with Mr. James in the Hopi country as a youth and did his first sketching there in the middle 1920's. Since then, because of the artistry and "feel" he possesses for authentic Indian portrayal, nearly every publisher of the books of Harry James has sought out this sensitive artist for their illustration.

During World War II Mr. Perceval served six years with the British navy, then returned to Southern California. His early interest in the Indians of the Southwest has continued, and they and their lands are the subject of many of his paintings. His artistry is amazingly versatile. He has illustrated books for many major publishers, and is aknowledged as one the greatest in this field. His home and studio are in Santa Barbara, California.

REPRINTED BY

MALKI MUSEUM PRESS

by arrangement with

SET IN LINOTYPE CALEDONIA

PRINTED ON WARREN NO. 66 ANTIQUE PAPER

AT WESTERNLORE PRESS

ART WORK BY DON LOUIS PERCEVAL